GUITAR PLAY-ALONG

HAL•LEONARD®

VOL. 185

AUDIO ACCESS INCLUDED

PLAYBACK+
Speed • Pitch • Balance • Loop

CONTENTS

2   Always With Me, Always With You

9   The Crush of Love

16   Flying in a Blue Dream

26   Friends

34   If I Could Fly

74   Starry Night

50   Summer Song

62   Surfing With the Alien

To access audio visit:
www.halleonard.com/mylibrary
Enter Code
6709-7034-1710-8867

Cover photo © Steve Jennings

ISBN 978-1-4950-0694-4

cherry lane
music company

EXCLUSIVELY DISTRIBUTED BY

HAL•LEONARD® CORPORATION

7777 W. BLUEMOUND RD. P.O. BOX 13819 MILWAUKEE, WI 53213

Visit Hal Leonard Online at
www.HalLeonard.com

Always With Me, Always With You

By Joe Satriani

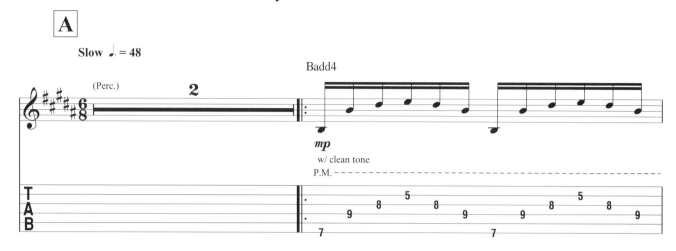

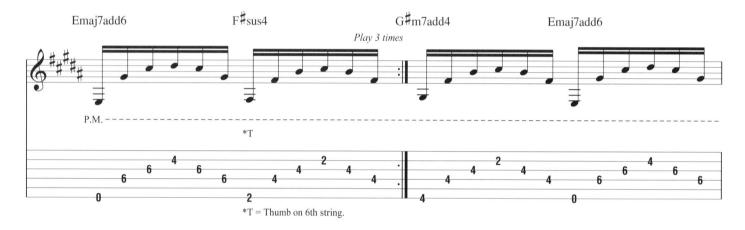

*T = Thumb on 6th string.

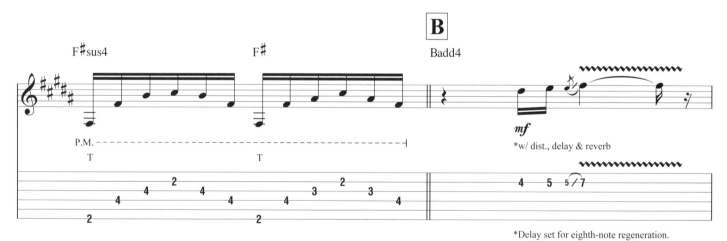

*Delay set for eighth-note regeneration.

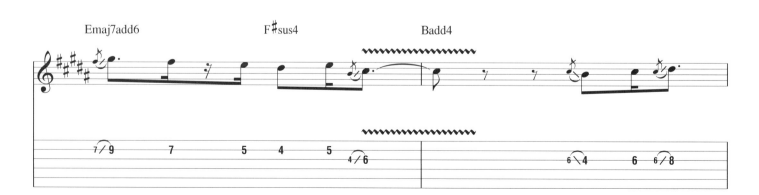

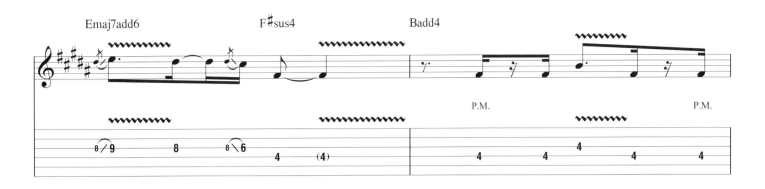

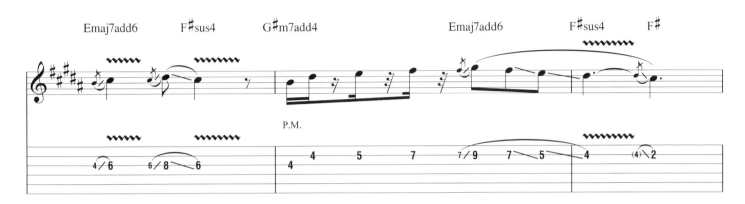

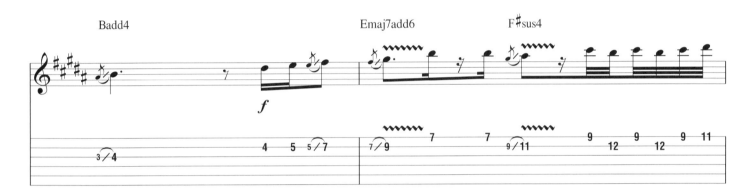

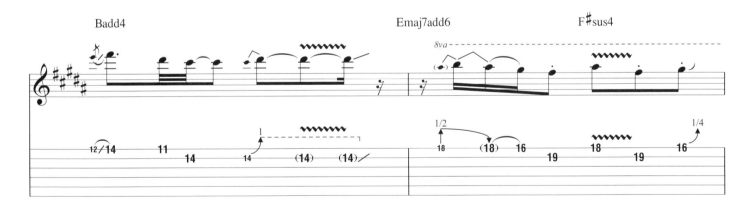

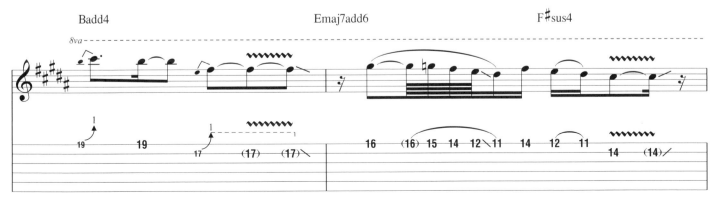

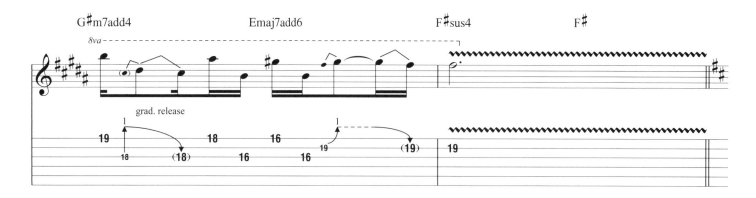

C

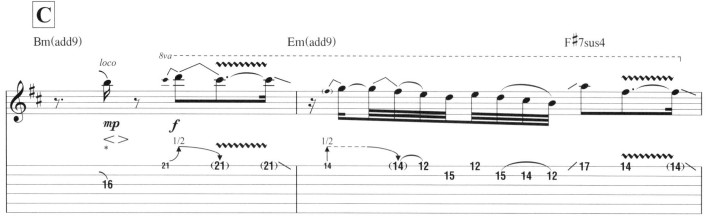

*Swell & fade w/ vol. knob.

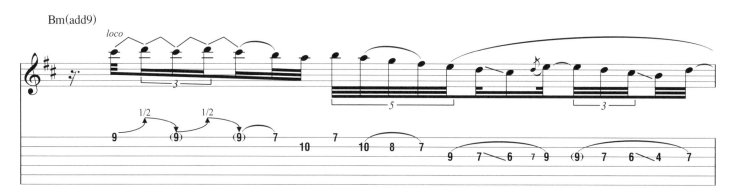

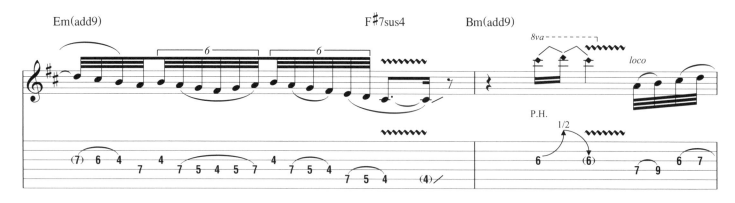

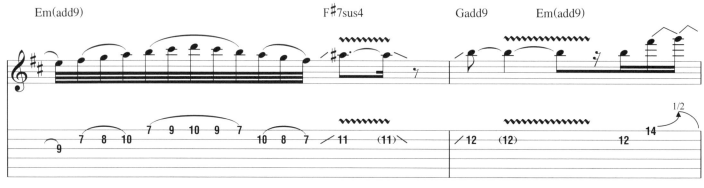

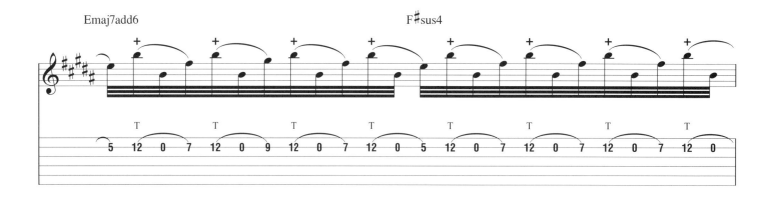

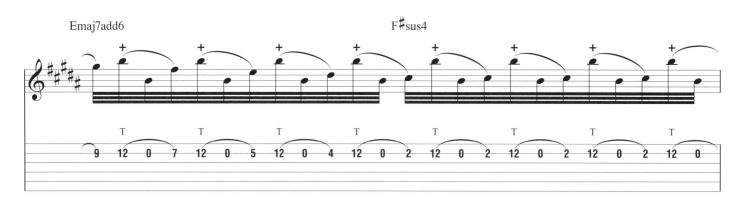

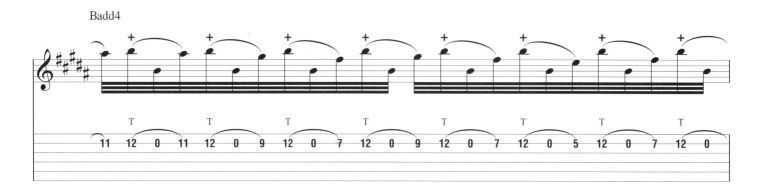

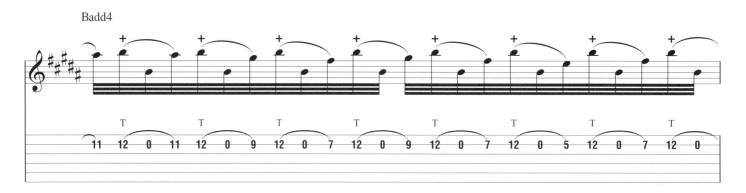

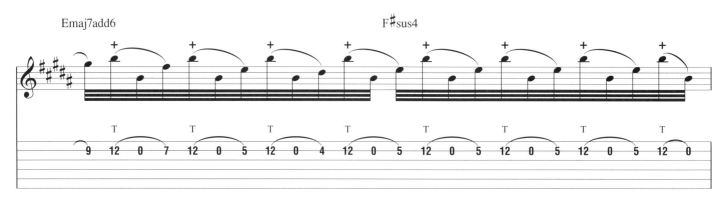

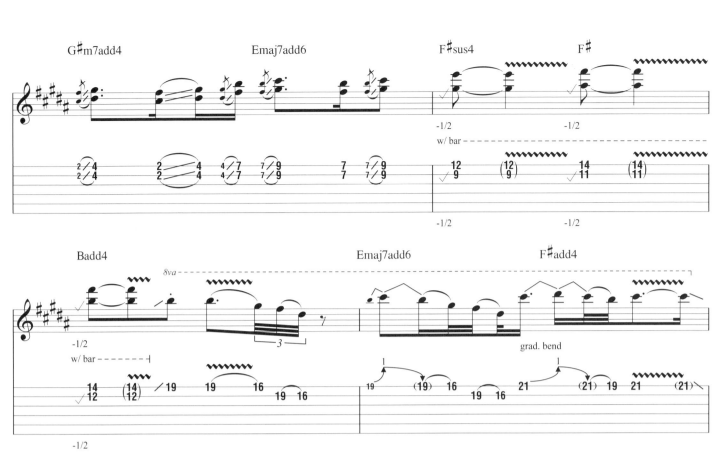

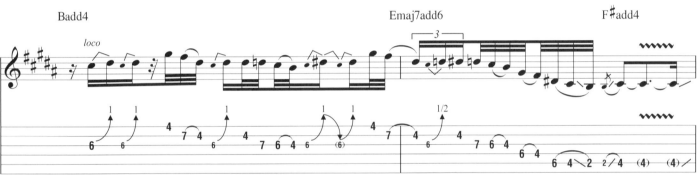

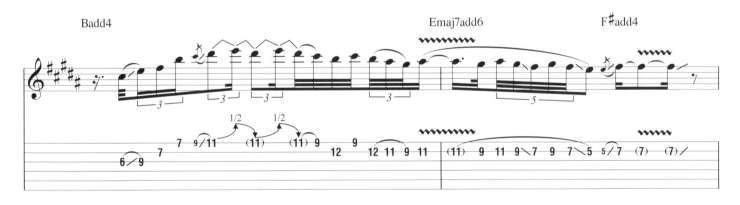

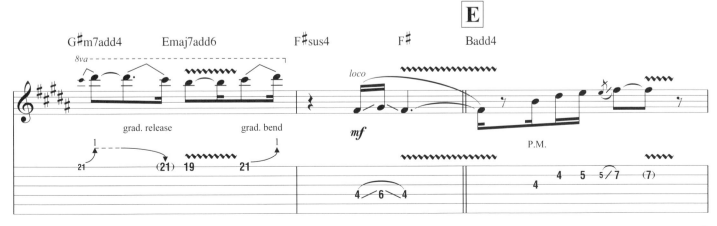

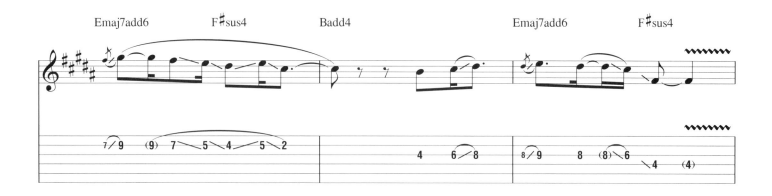

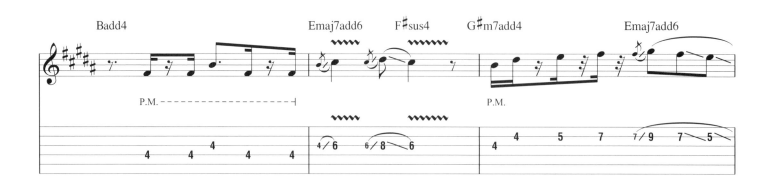

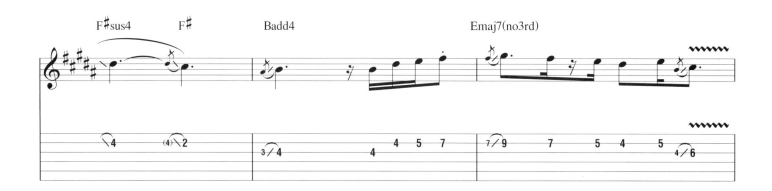

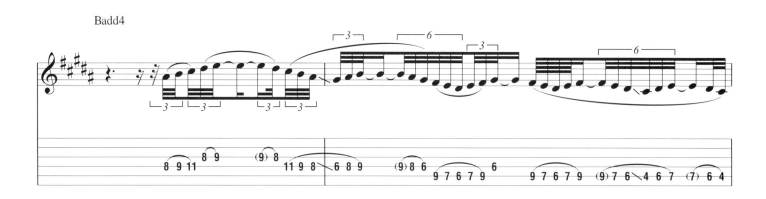

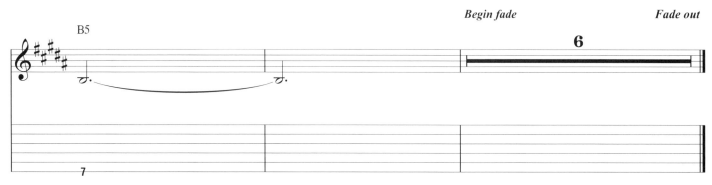

The Crush of Love

By Joe Satriani

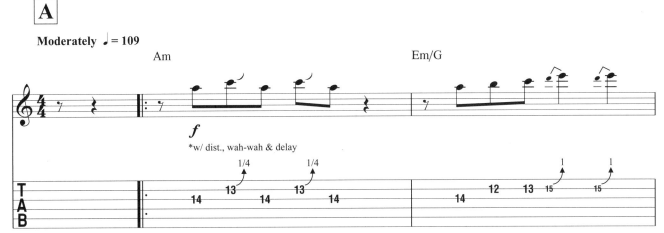

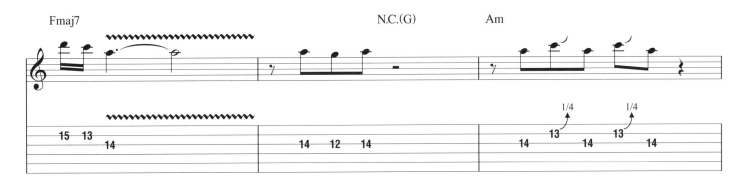

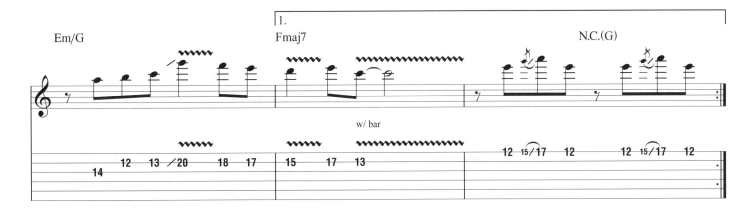

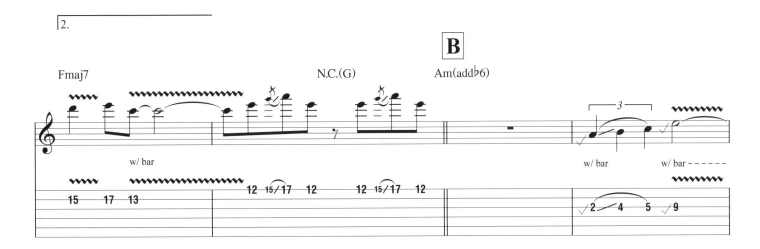

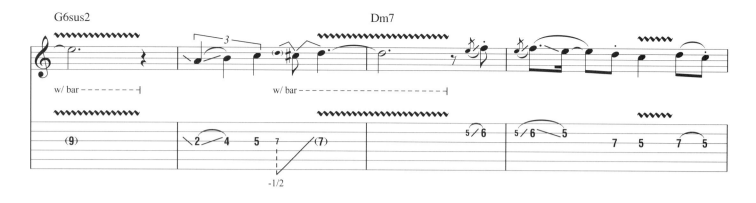

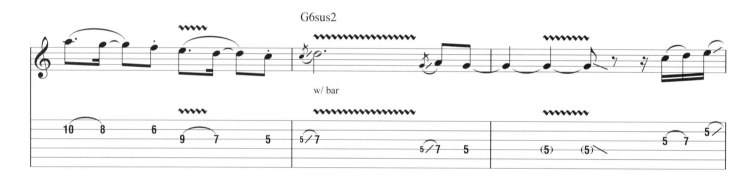

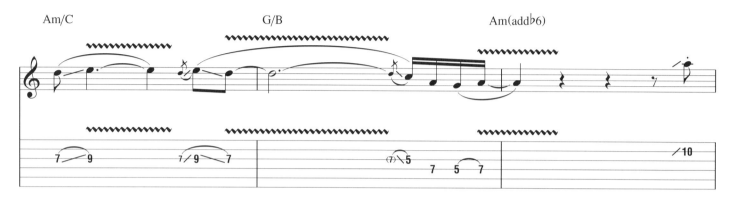

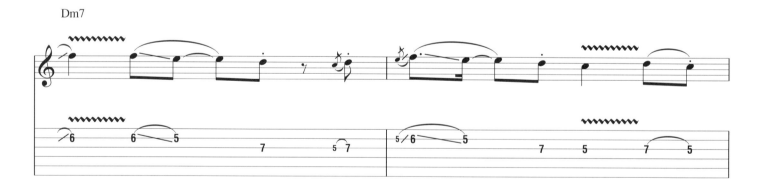

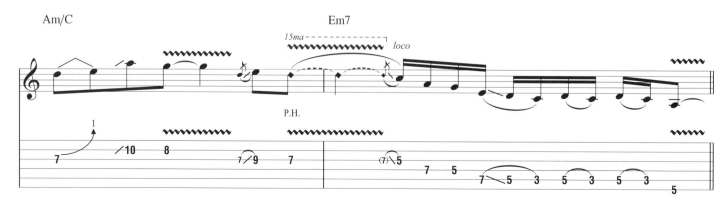

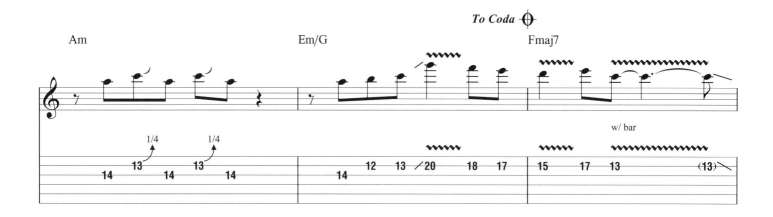

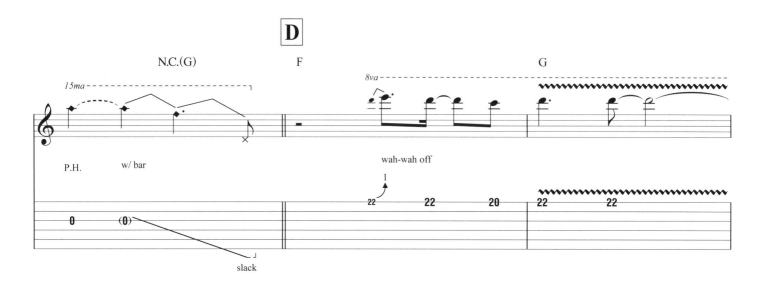

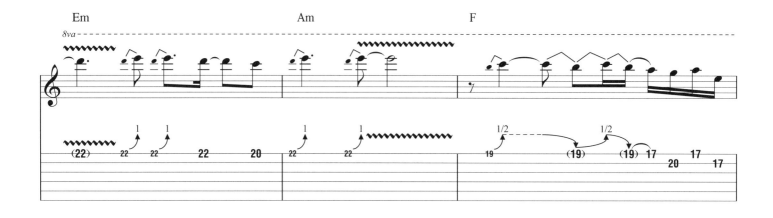

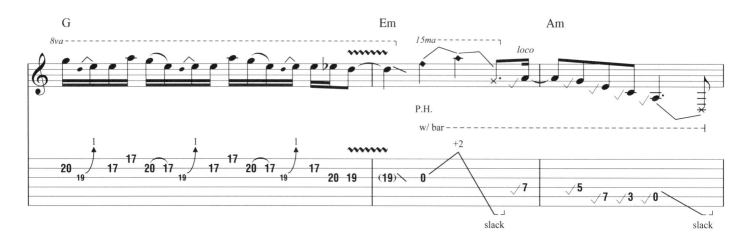

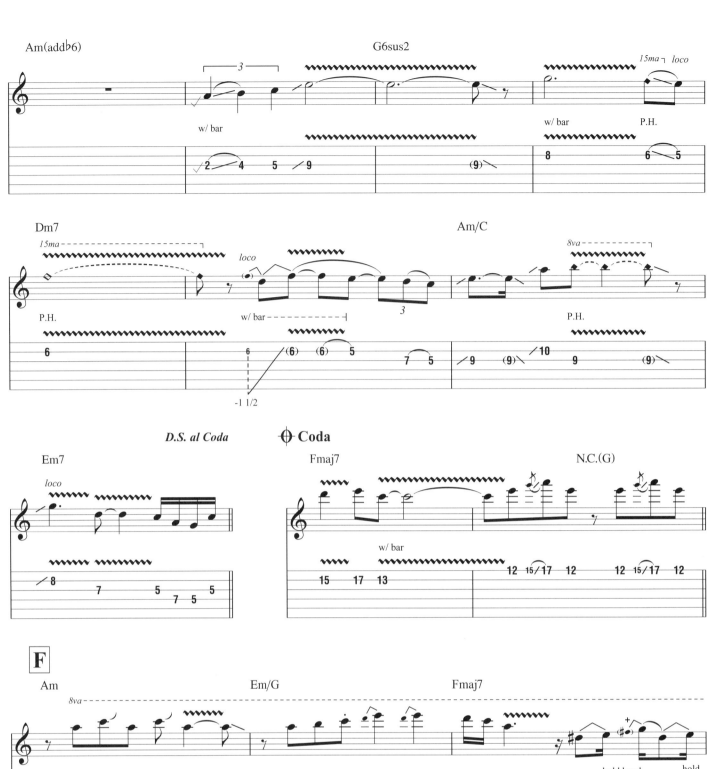

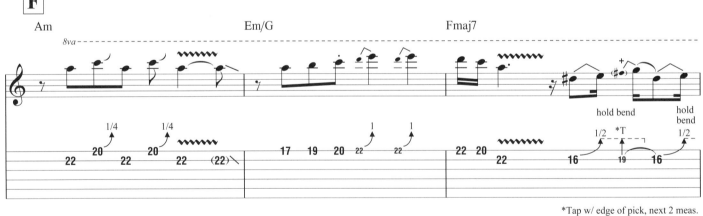

*Tap w/ edge of pick, next 2 meas.

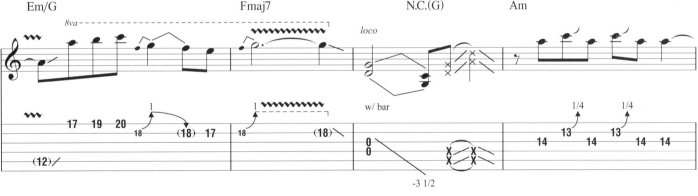

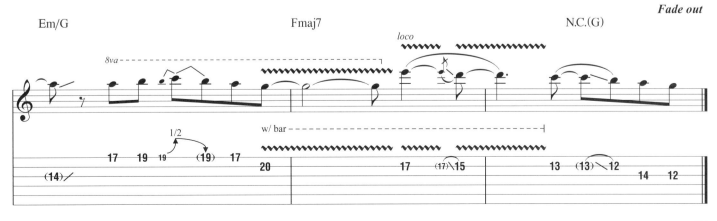

Flying in a Blue Dream

By Joe Satriani

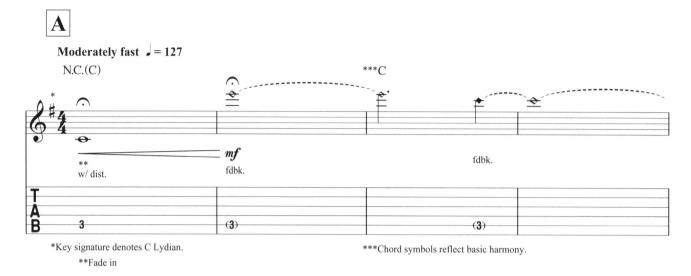

*Key signature denotes C Lydian.

**Fade in

***Chord symbols reflect basic harmony.

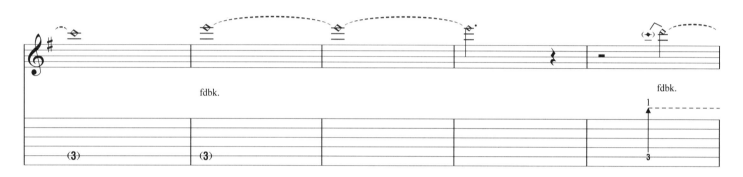

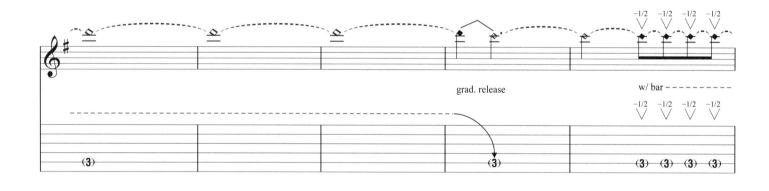

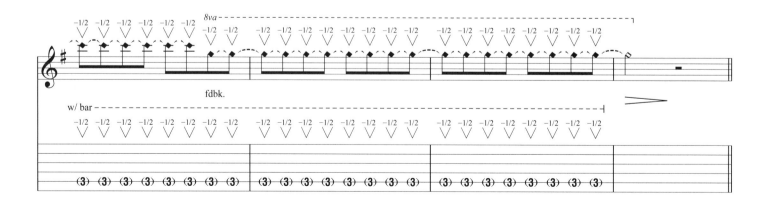

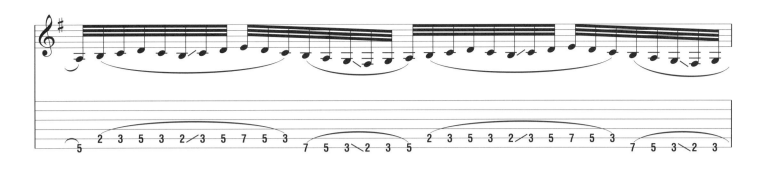

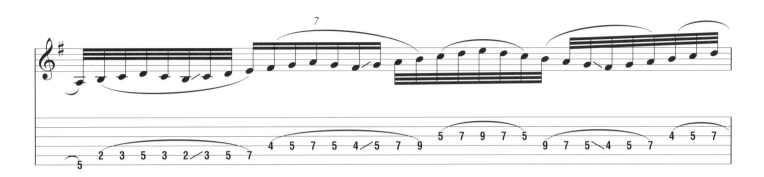

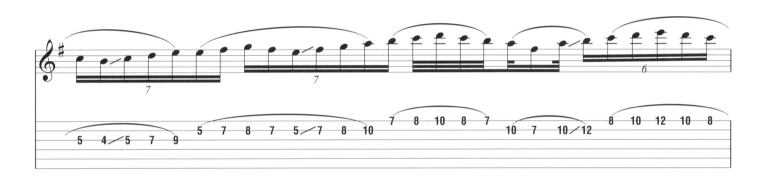

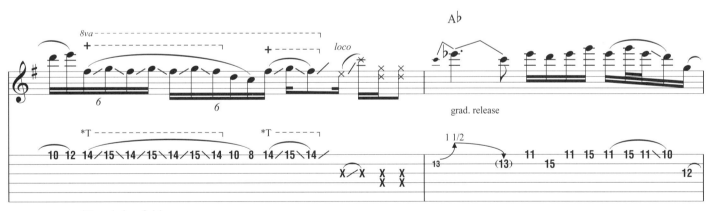

*Tap w/ edge of pick.

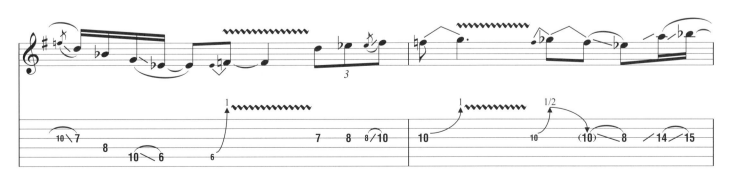

C

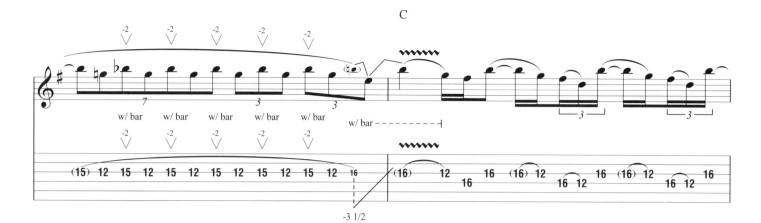

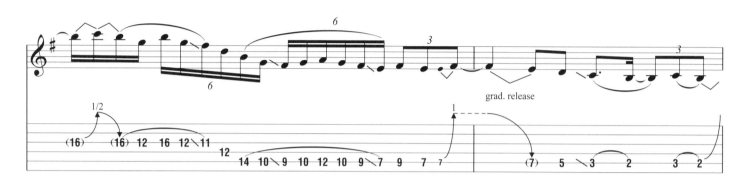

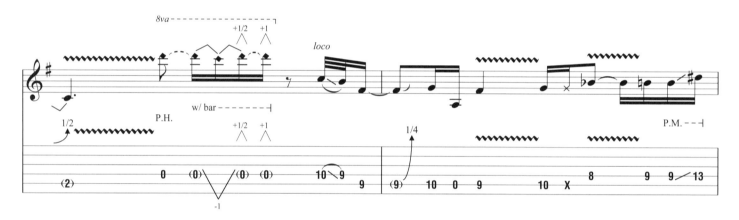

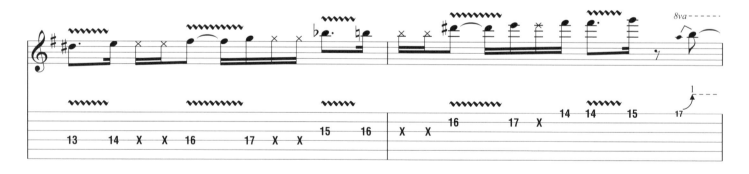

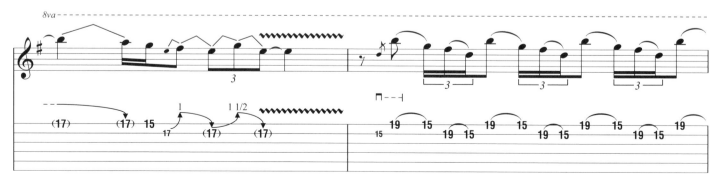

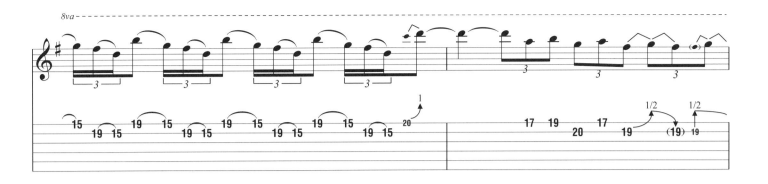

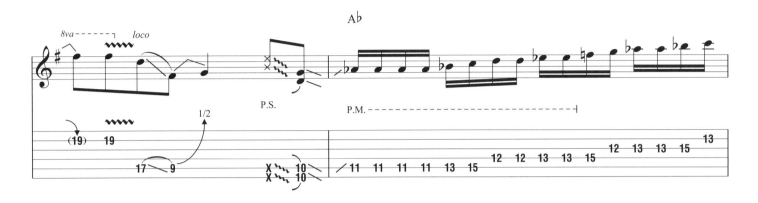

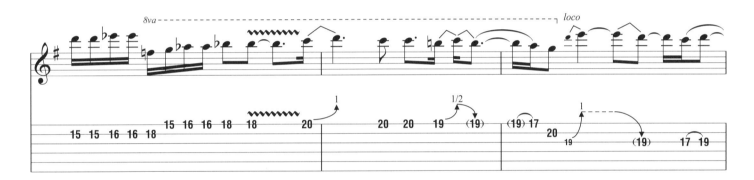

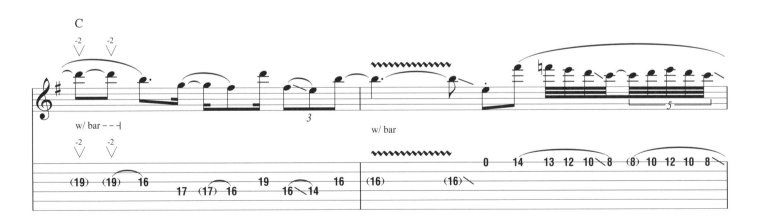

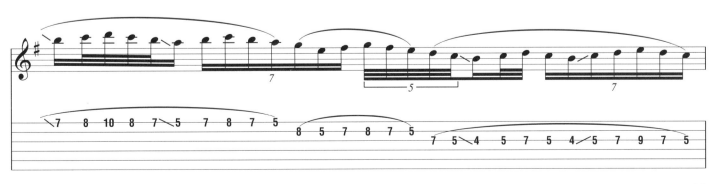

D

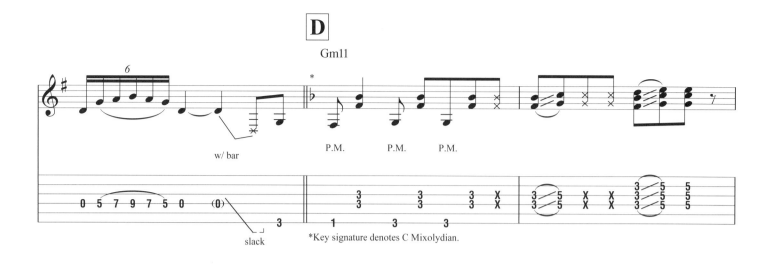

*Key signature denotes C Mixolydian.

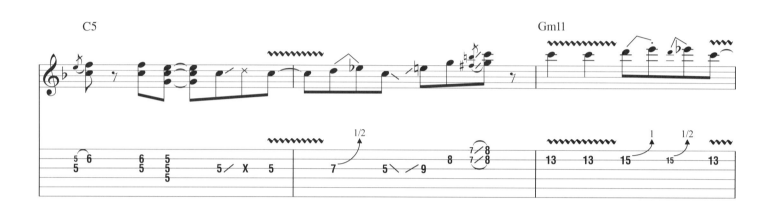

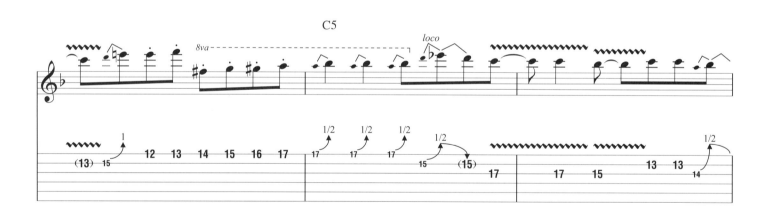

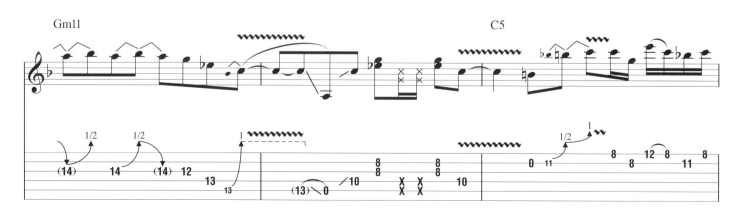

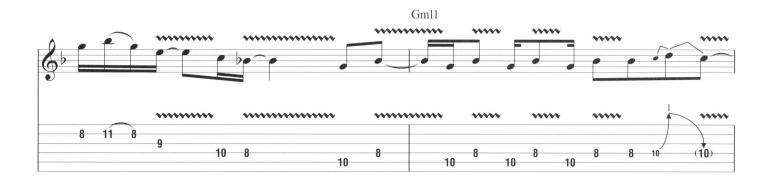

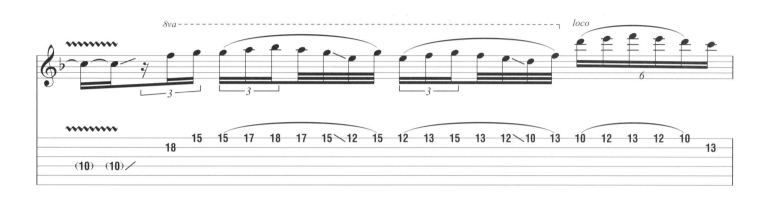

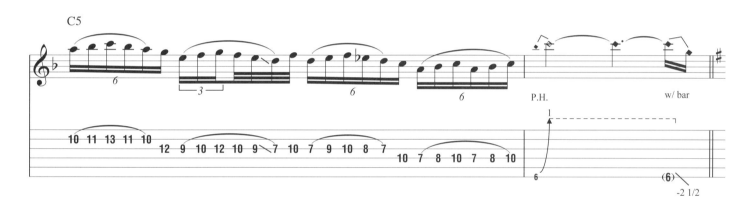

*Key signature denotes C Lydian.

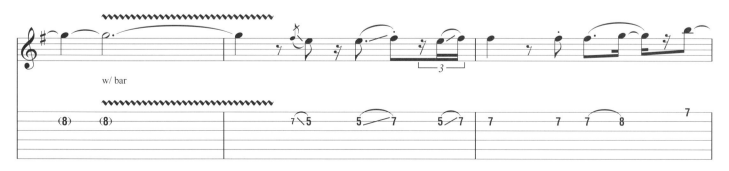

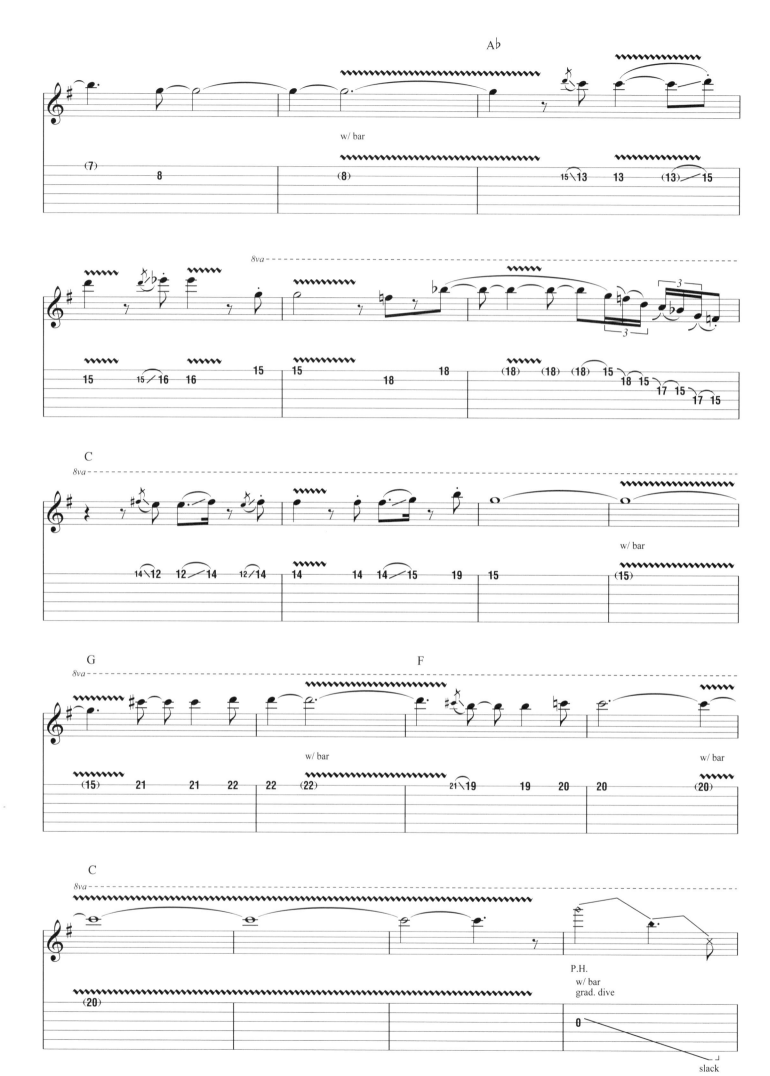

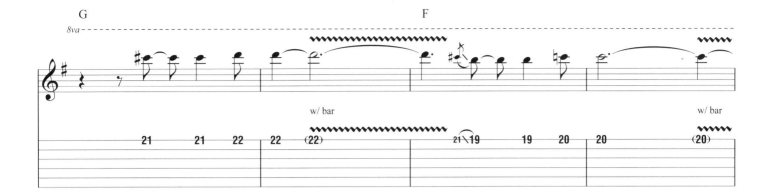

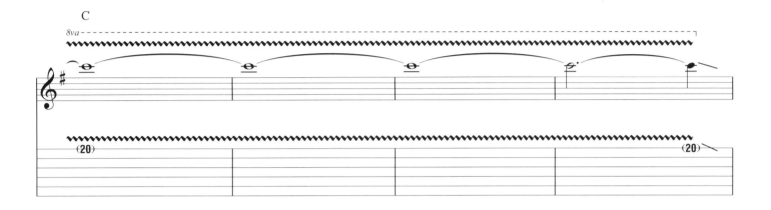

Friends

By Joe Satriani and Andy Johns

Drop D tuning, down 1/2 step:
(low to high) D♭-A♭-D♭-G♭-B♭-E♭

Moderately ♩ = 86

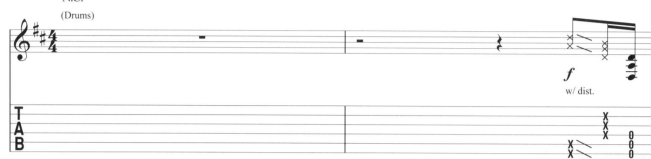

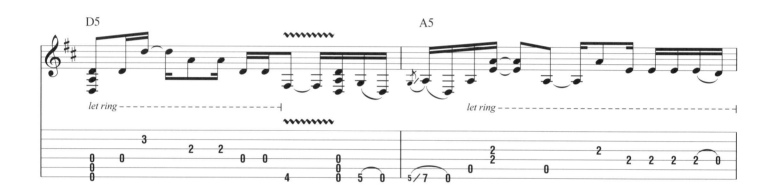

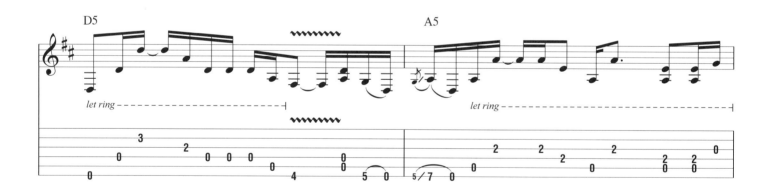

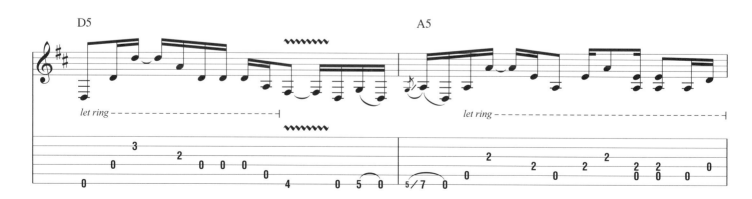

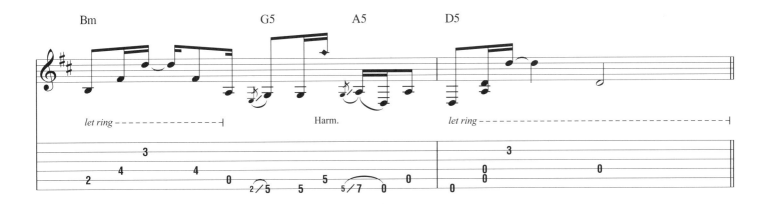

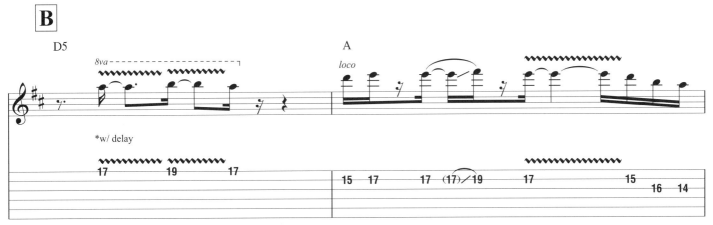

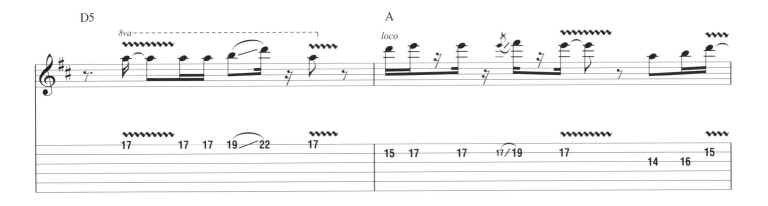

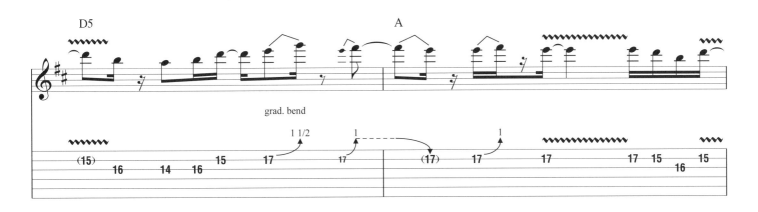

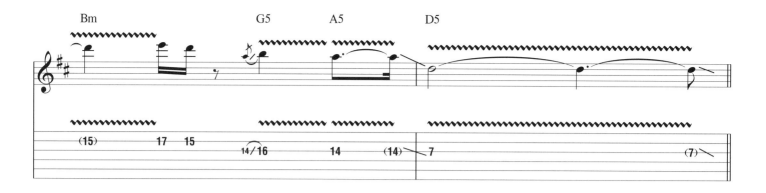

C

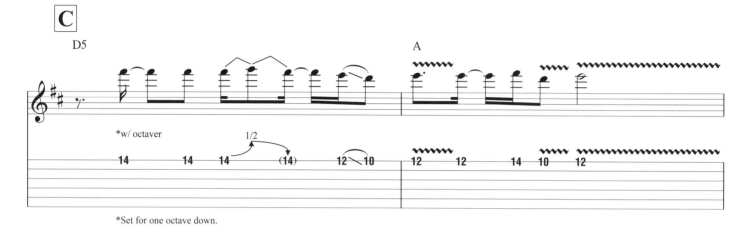

*w/ octaver

*Set for one octave down.

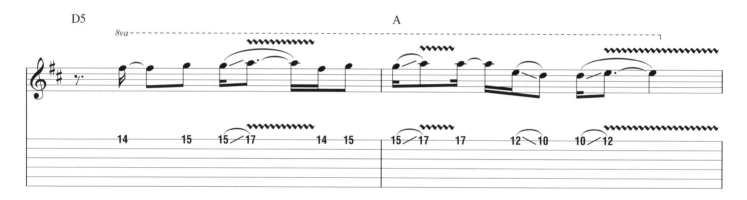

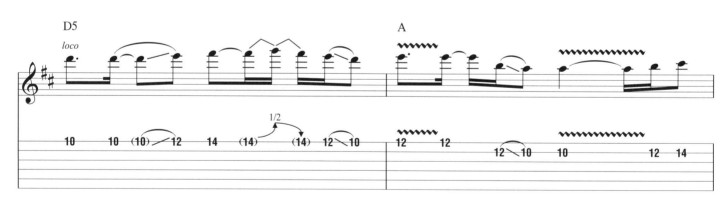

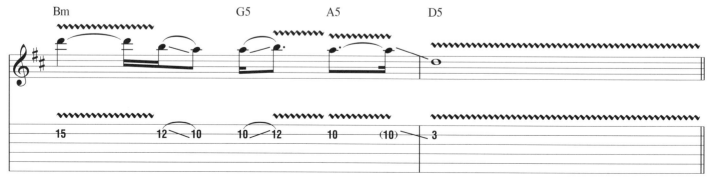

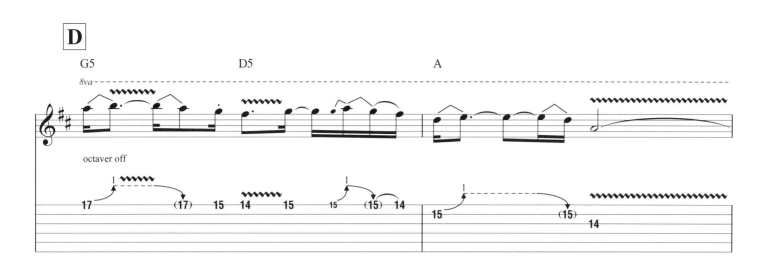

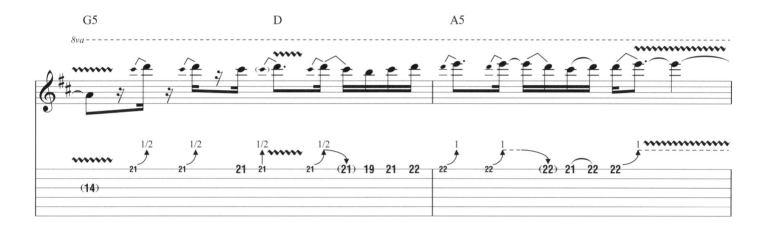

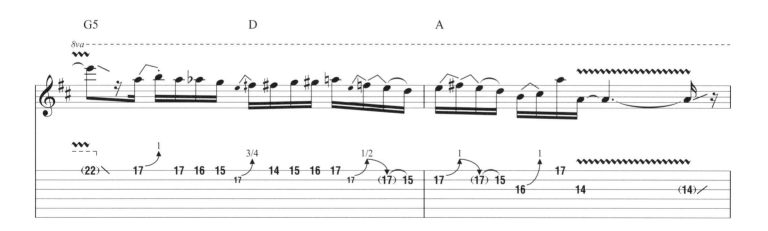

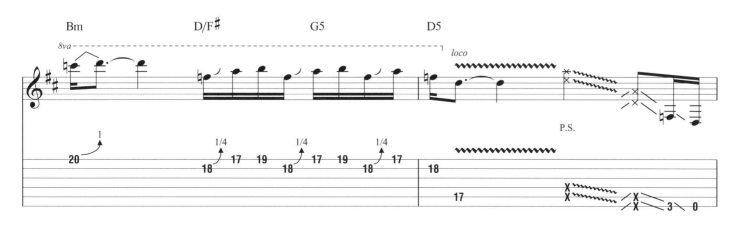

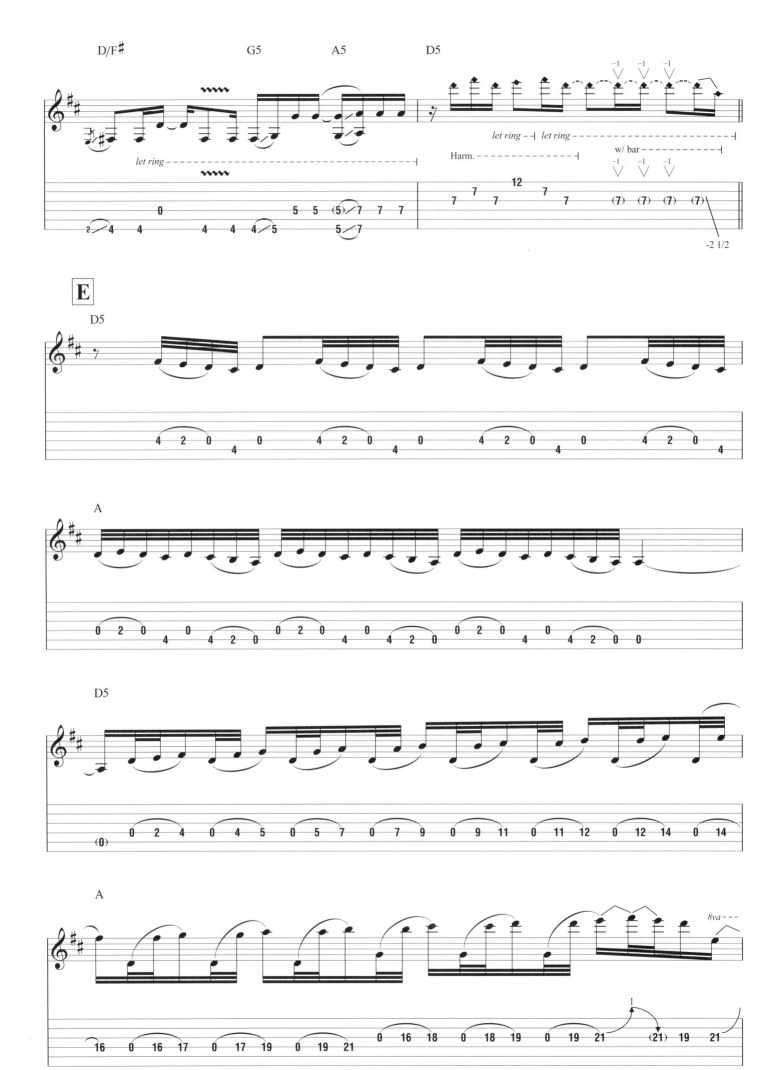

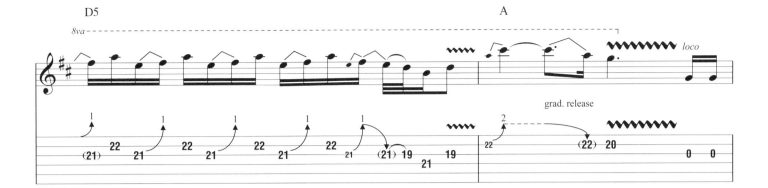

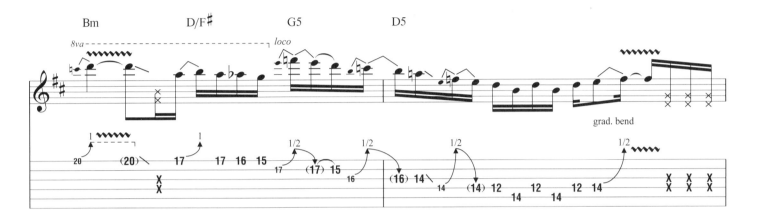

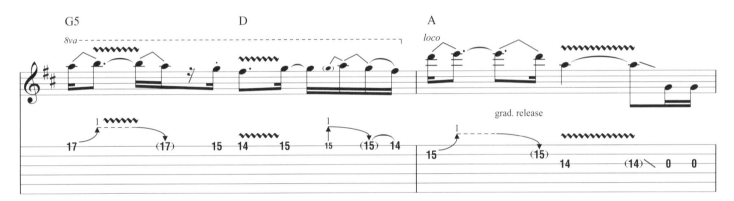

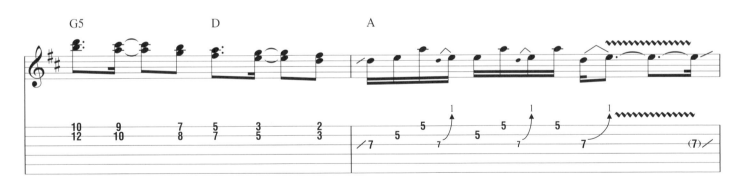

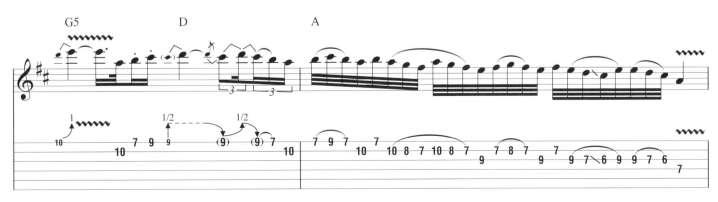

If I Could Fly

By Joe Satriani

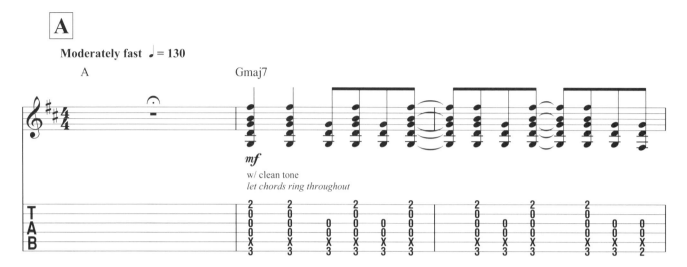

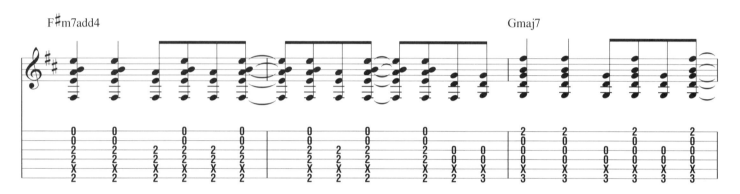

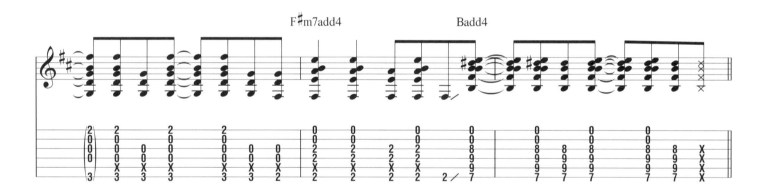

*Delay set for quarter-note regeneration.

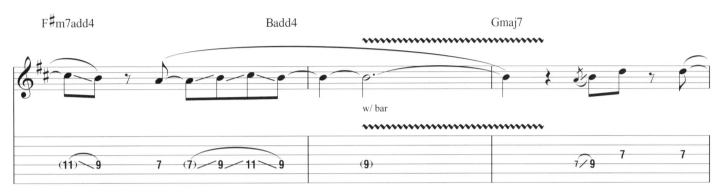

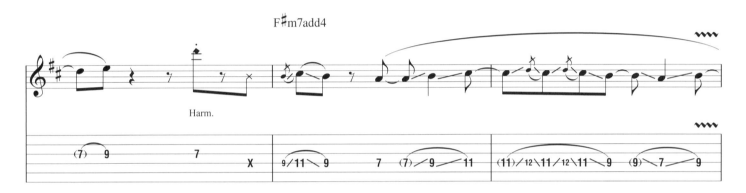

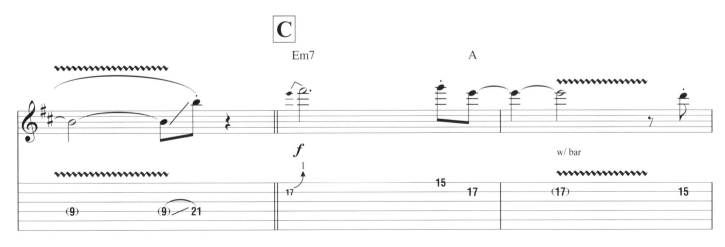

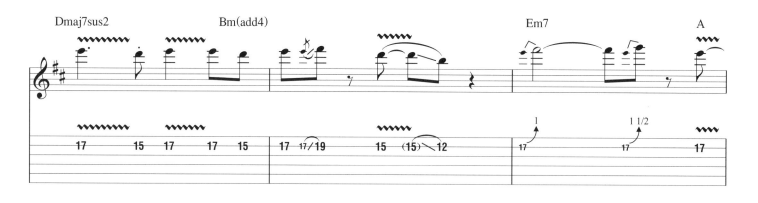

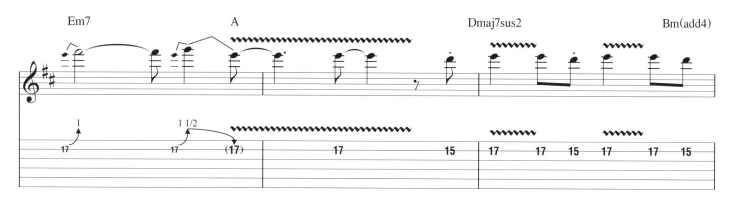

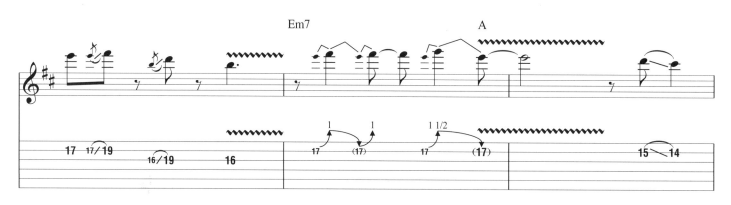

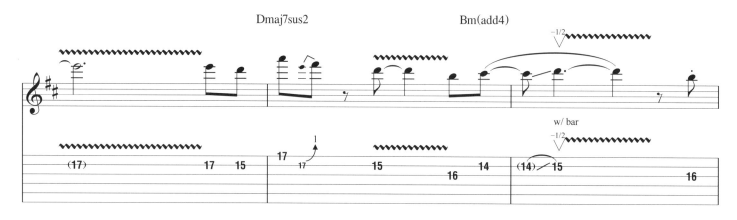

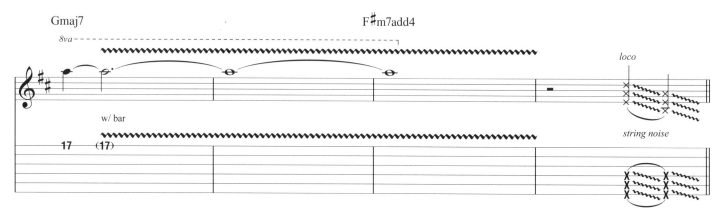

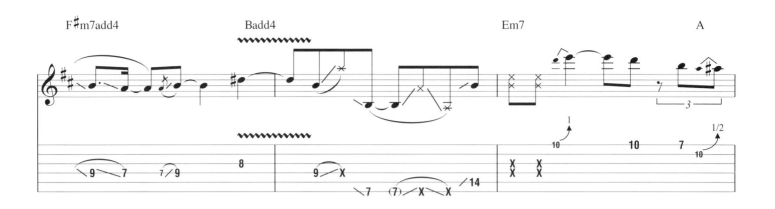

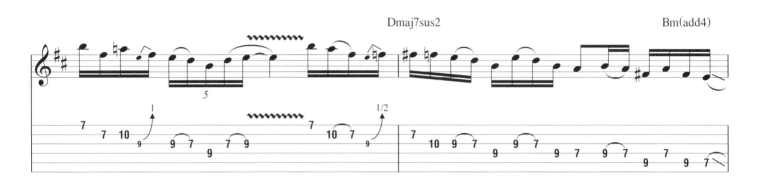

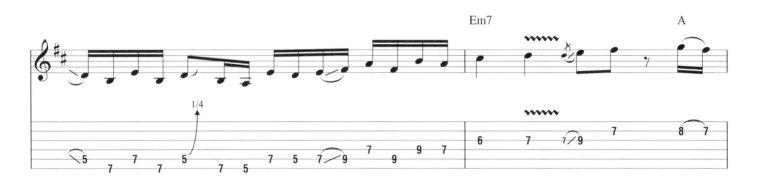

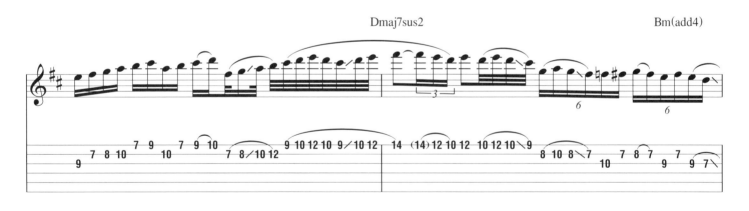

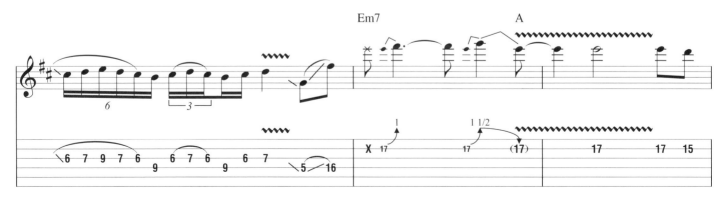

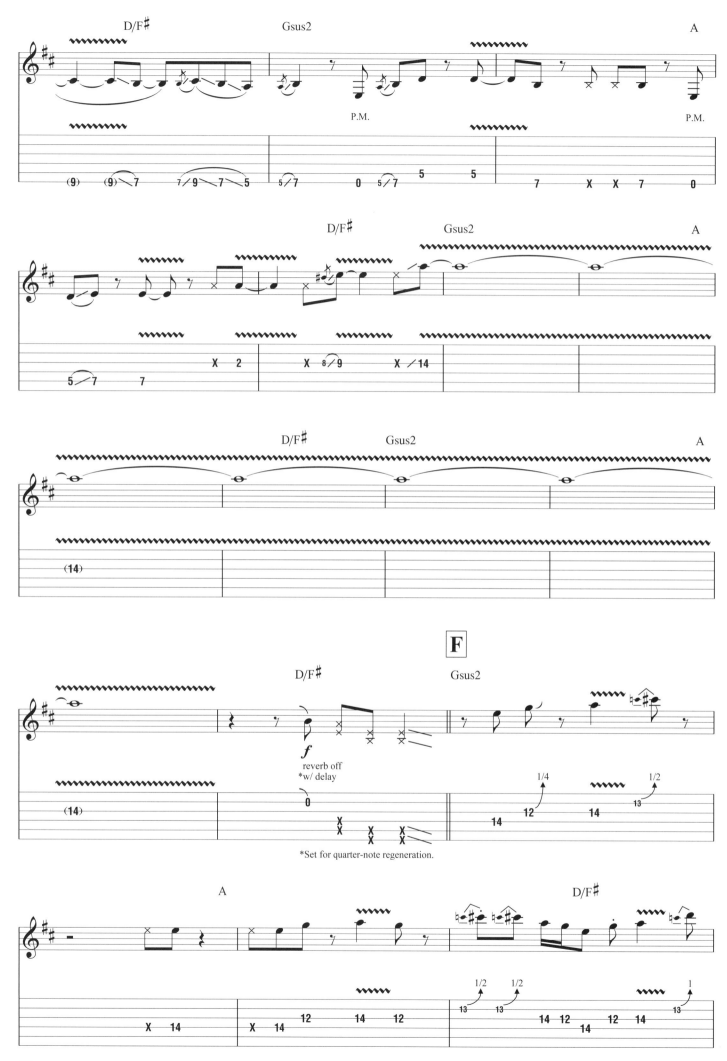

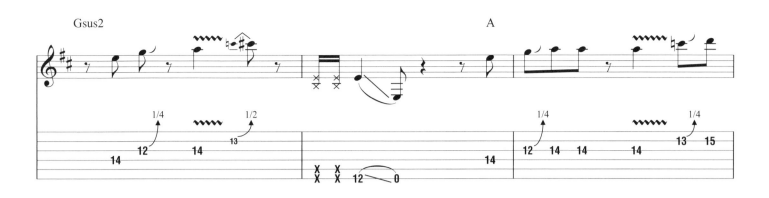

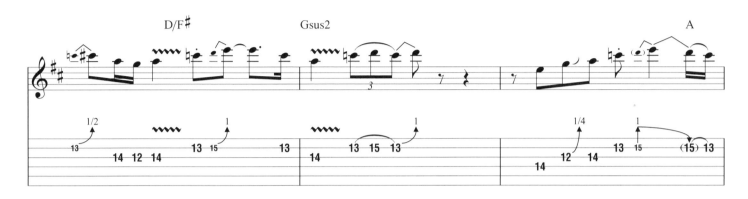

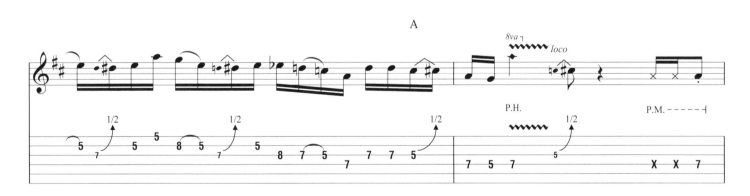

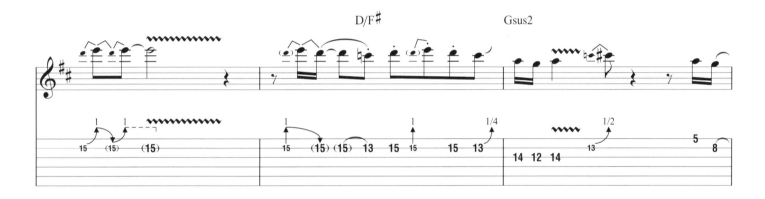

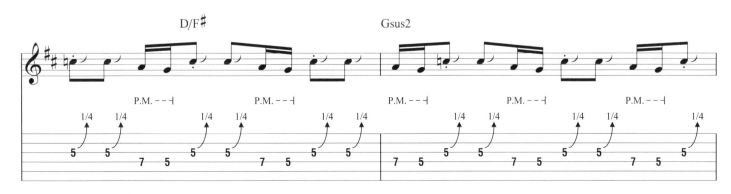

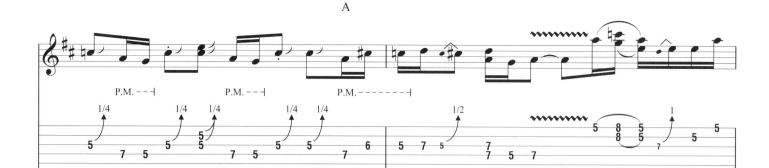

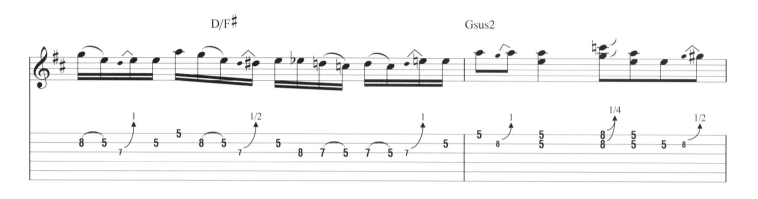

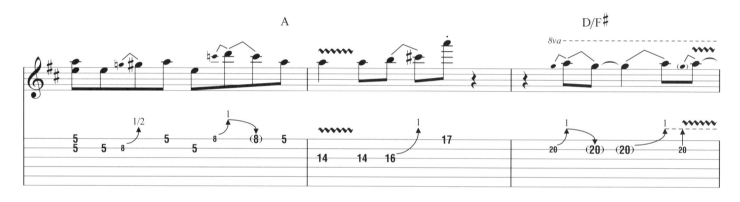

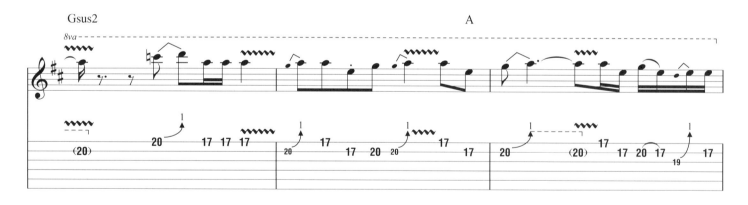

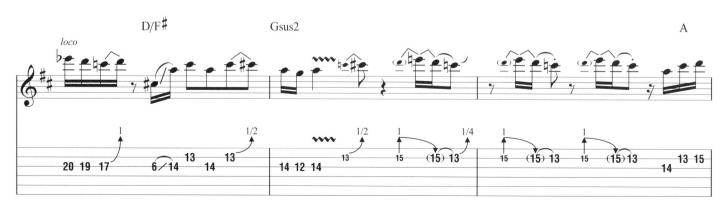

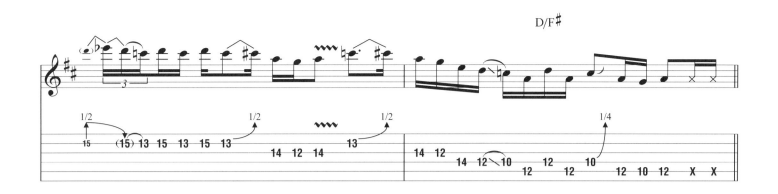

G

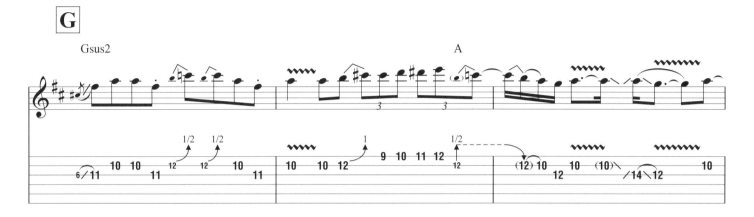

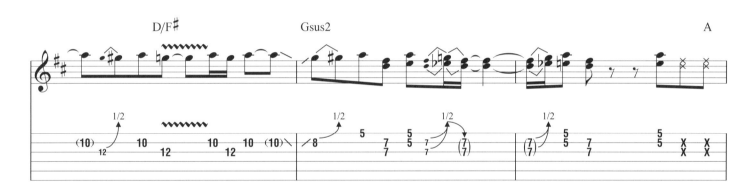

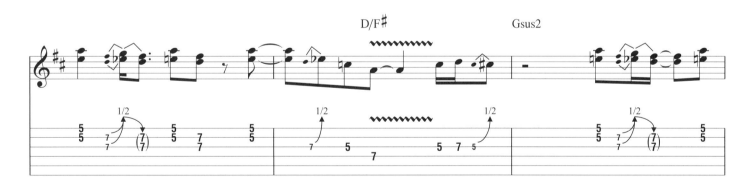

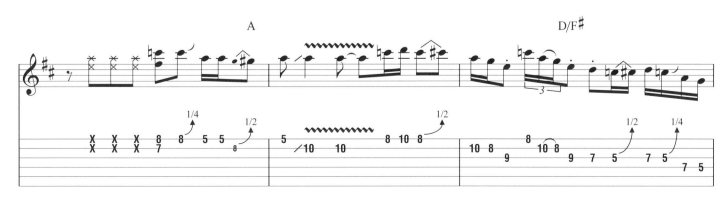

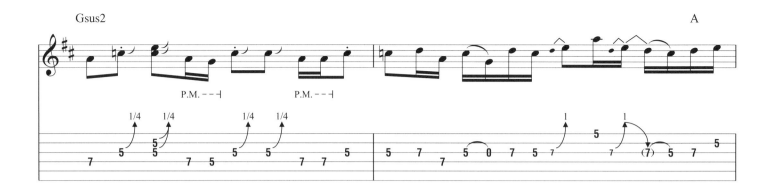

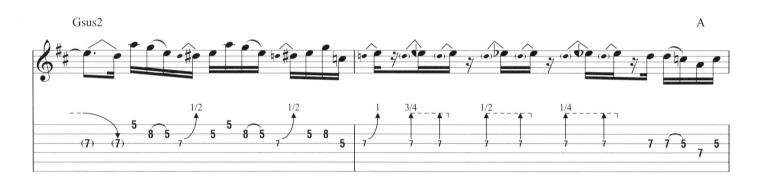

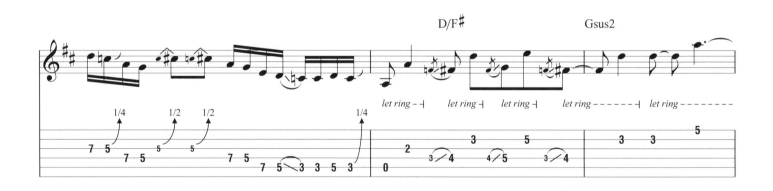

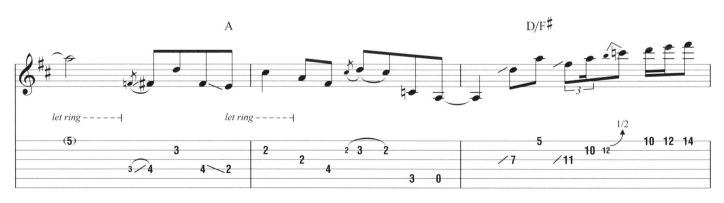

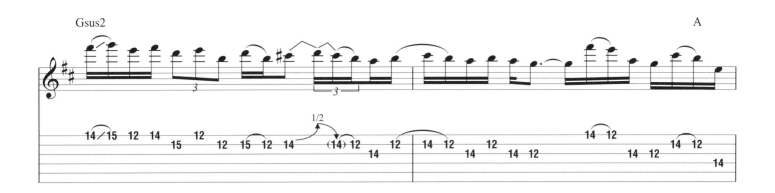

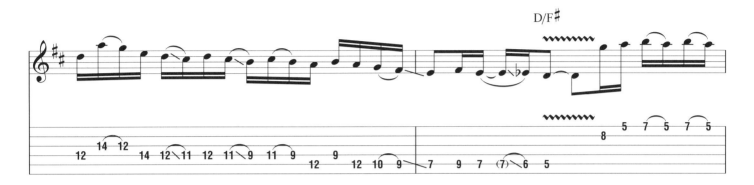

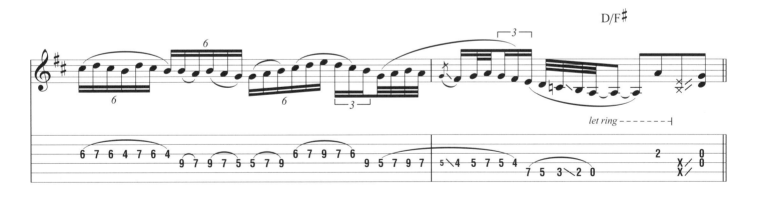

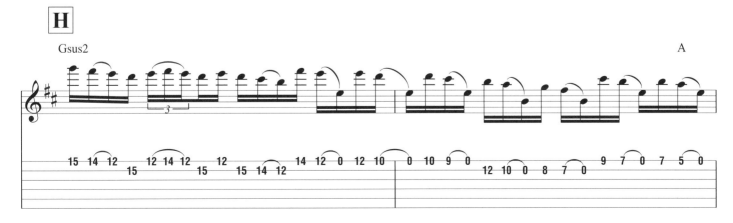

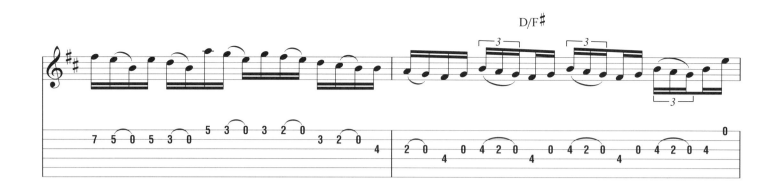

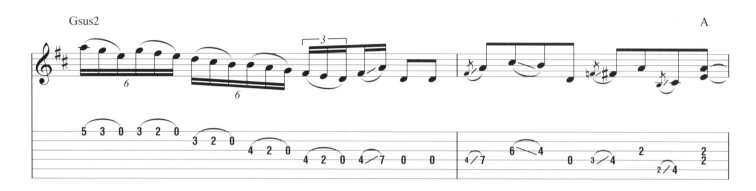

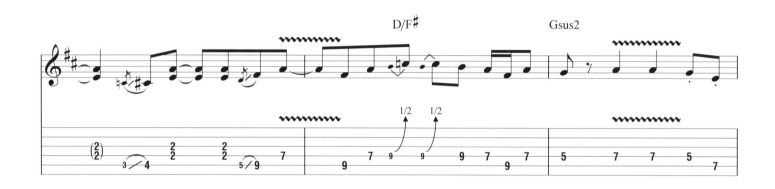

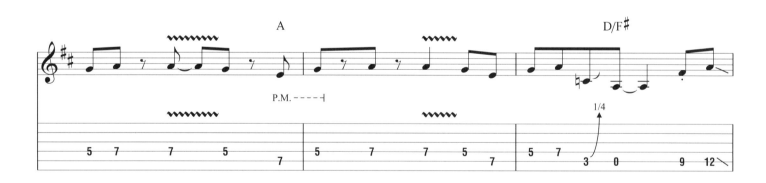

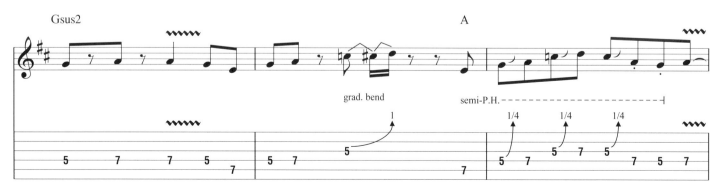

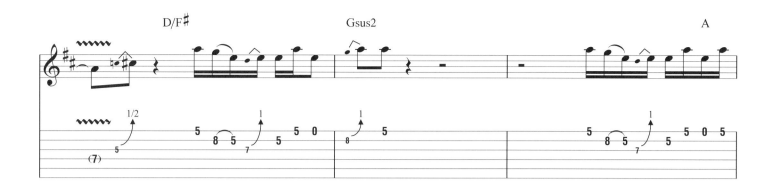

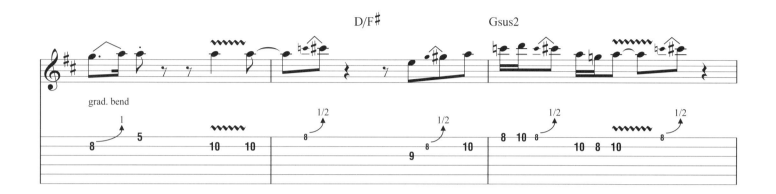

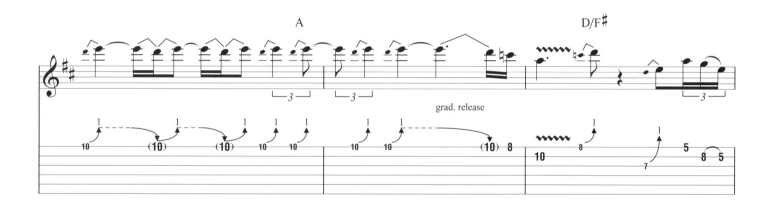

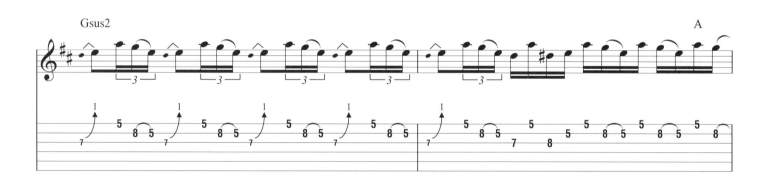

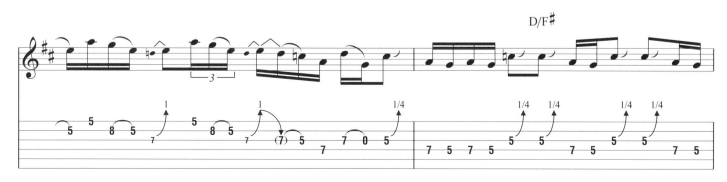

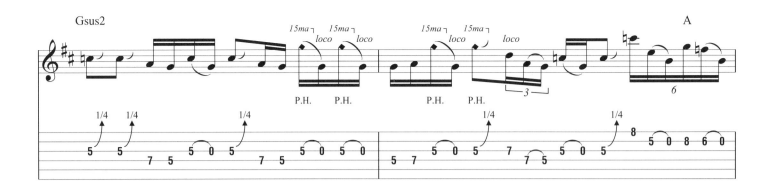

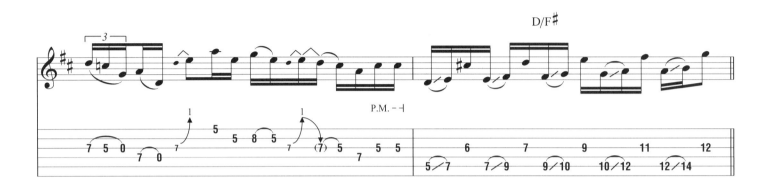

I

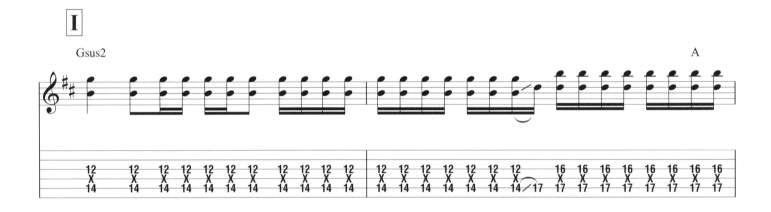

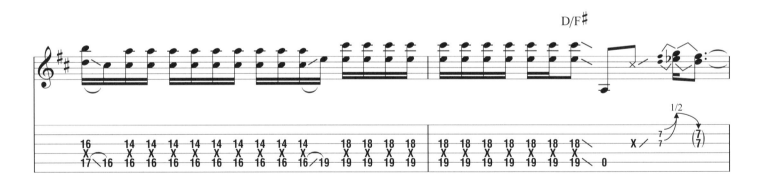

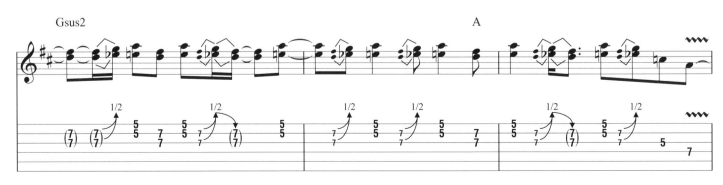

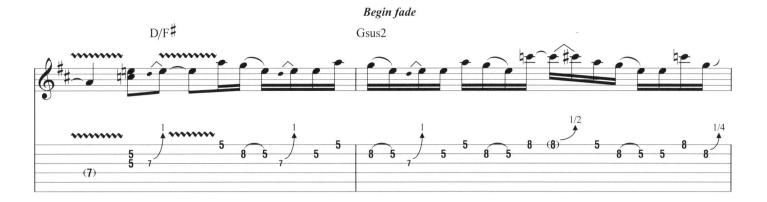

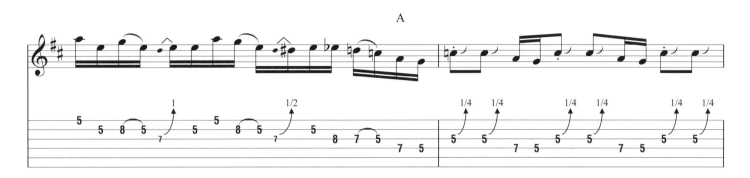

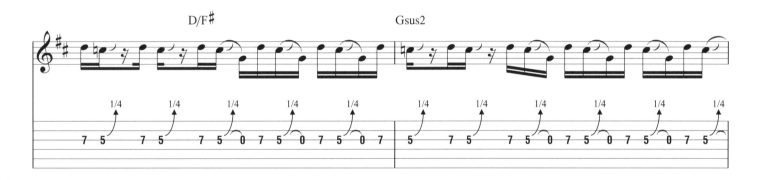

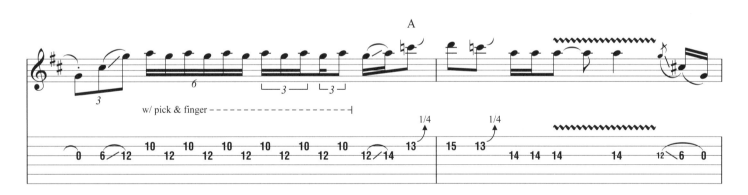

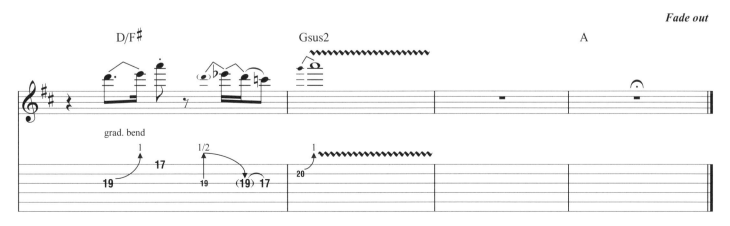

Summer Song

By Joe Satriani

Moderately fast ♩ = 162

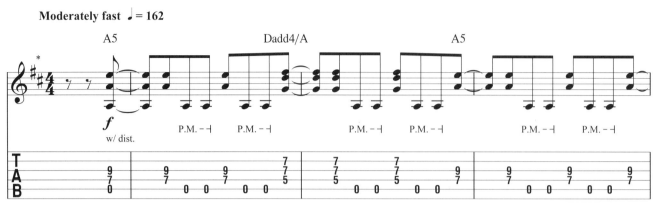

*Key signature denotes A Mixolydian.

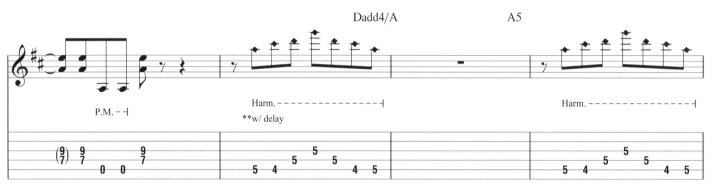

**Stereo delay set for 1 1/2-beat & 2 1/2-beat regeneration.

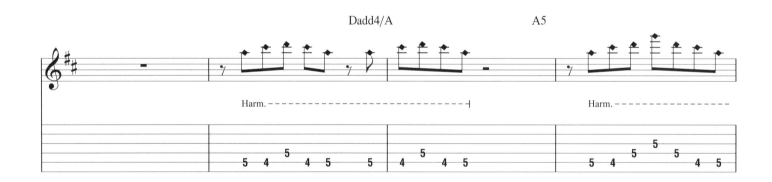

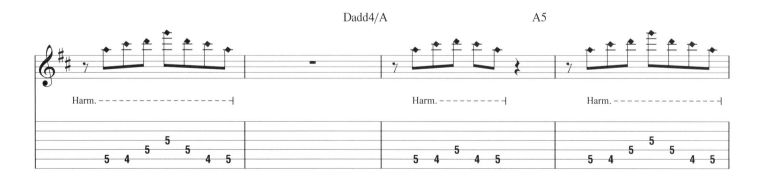

B

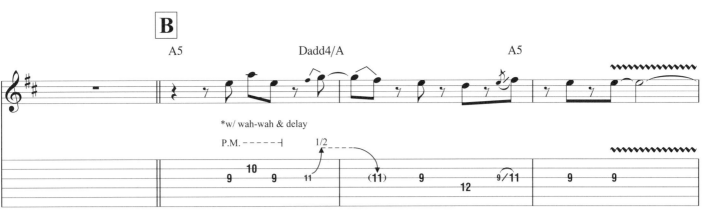

*w/ wah-wah & delay

*Delay set for quarter-note regeneration.

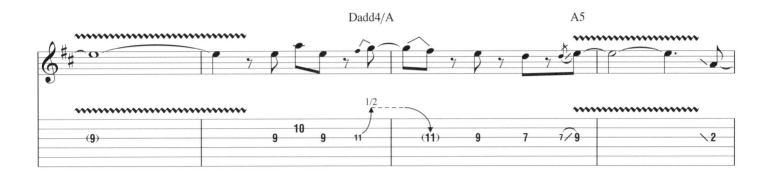

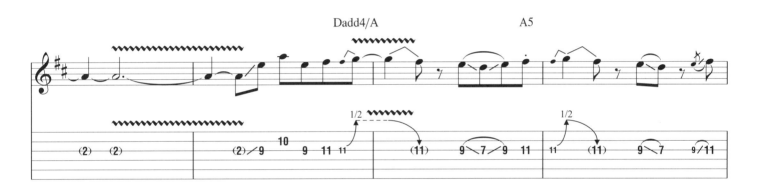

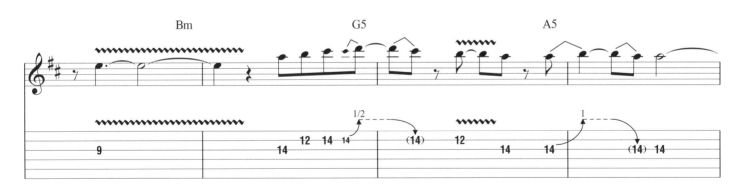

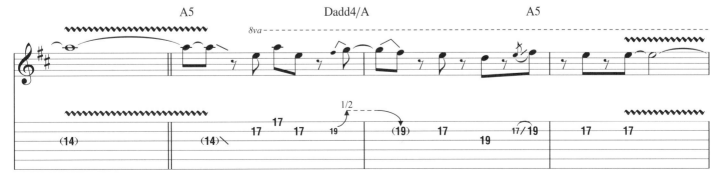

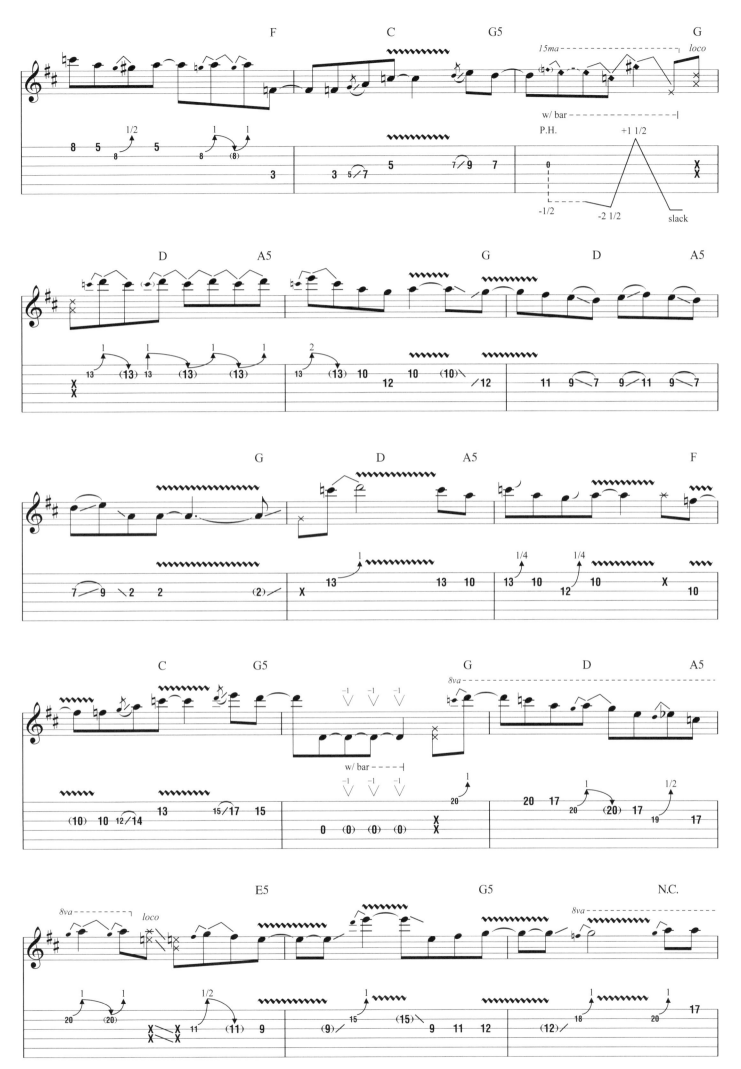

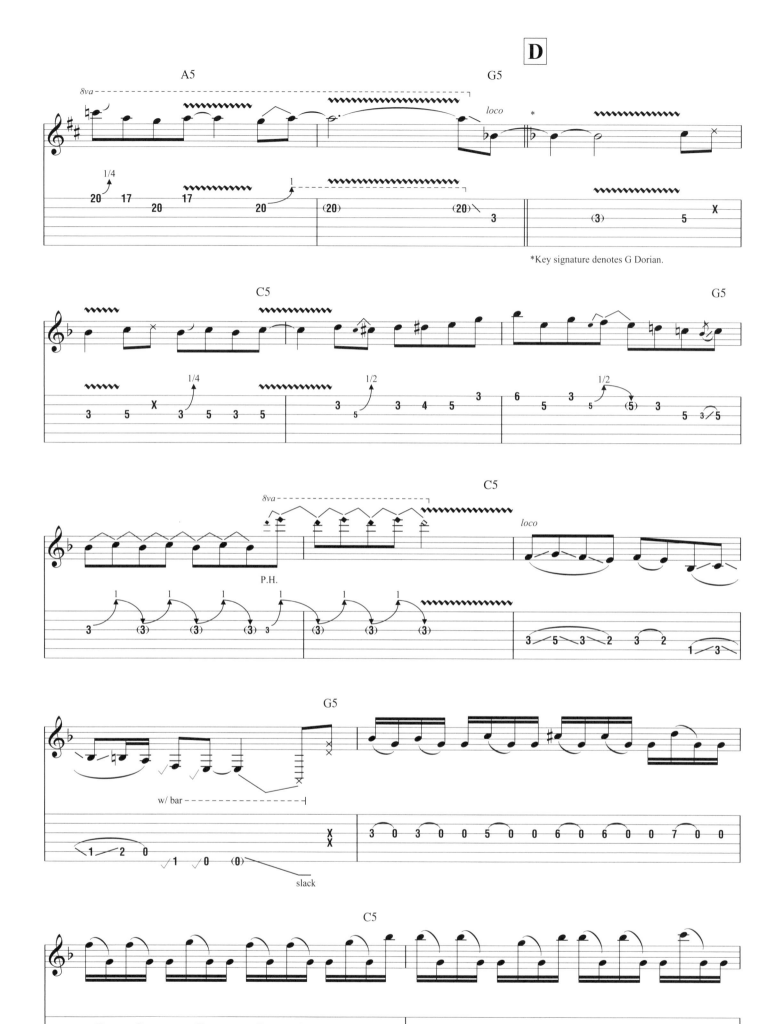

*Key signature denotes G Dorian.

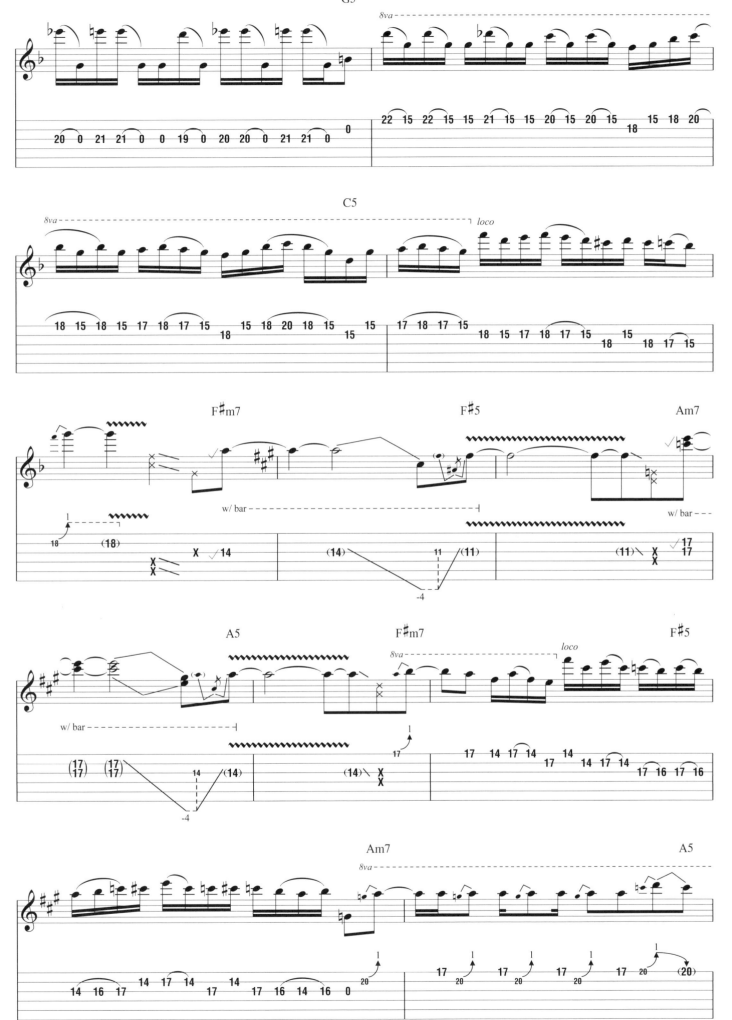

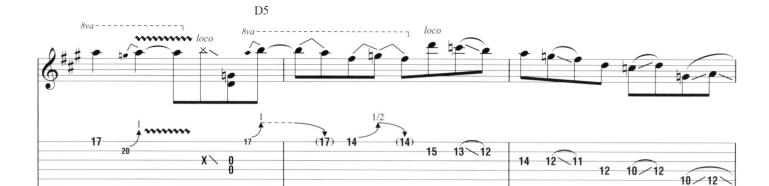

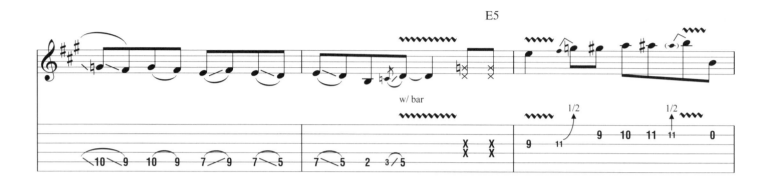

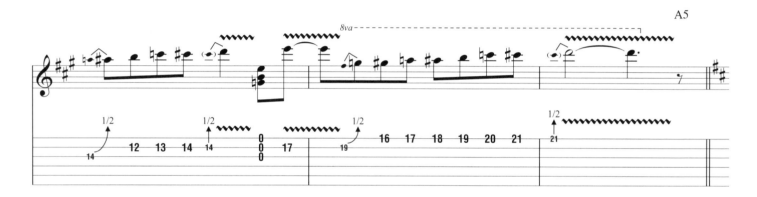

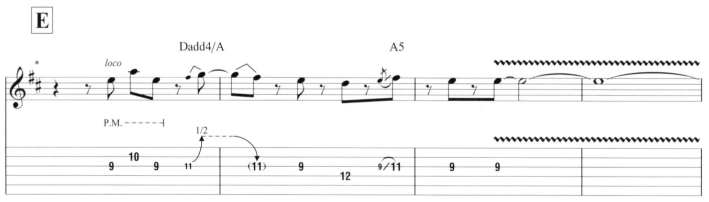

*Key signature denotes A Mixolydian.

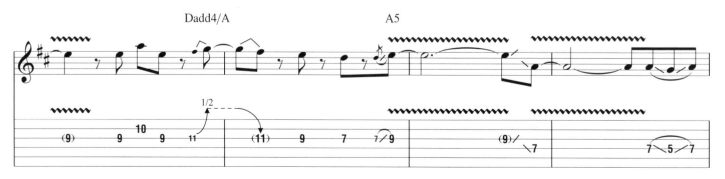

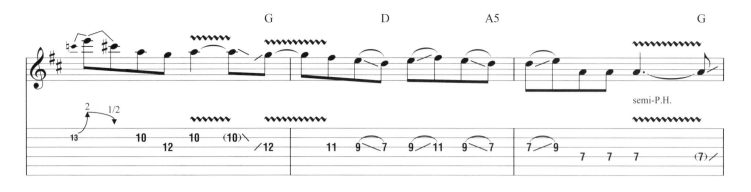

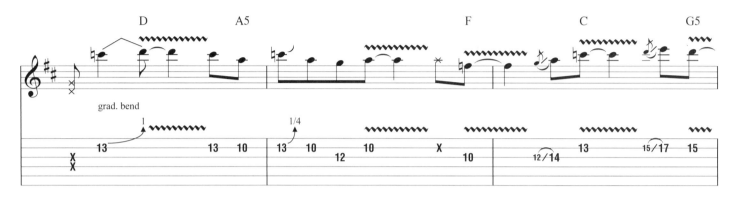

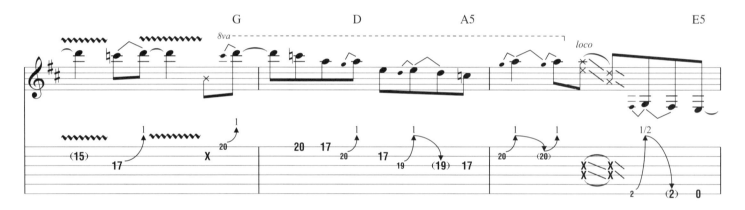

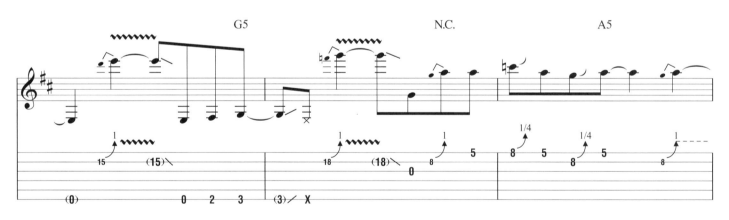

G

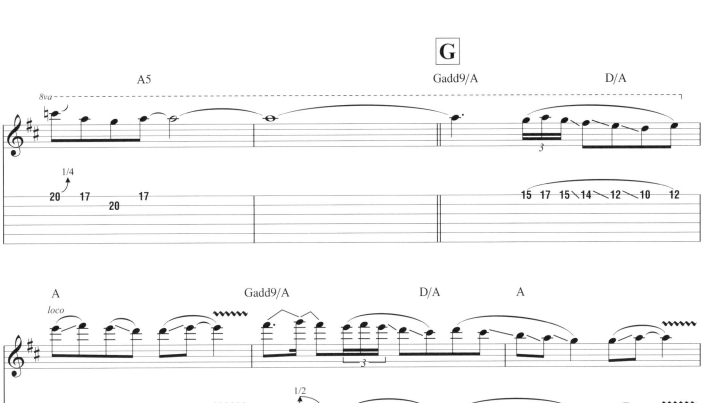

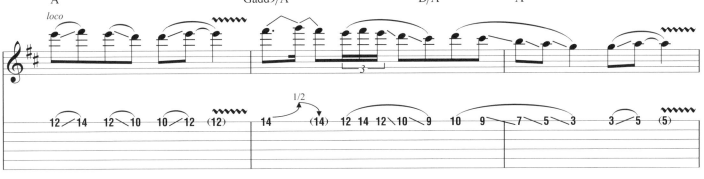

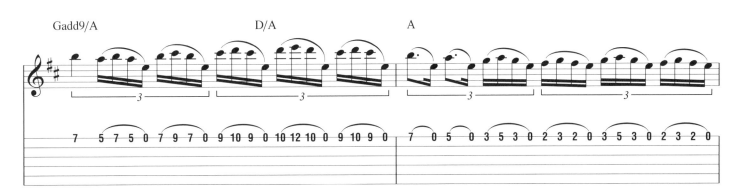

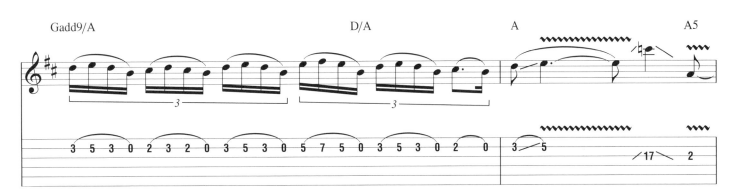

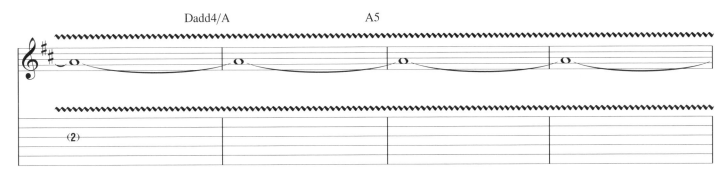

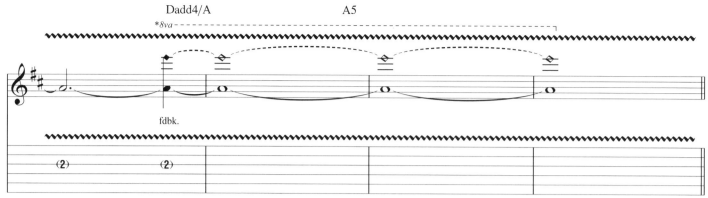

Dadd4/A   A5

*Applies to fdbk. pitch only.

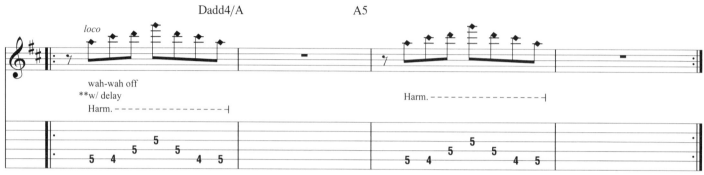

Dadd4/A   A5

wah-wah off
**w/ delay
Harm. - - - - - - - - - - - -

Harm. - - - - - - - - - - - -

**Stereo delay as before.

H

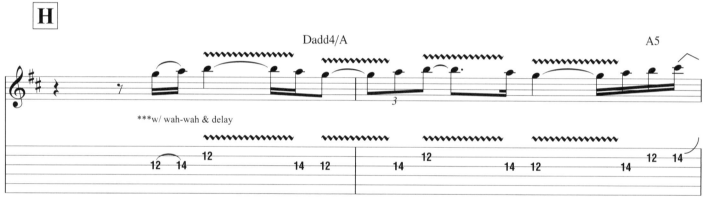

Dadd4/A   A5

***w/ wah-wah & delay

***Delay set for quarter-note regeneration.

semi-P.H.

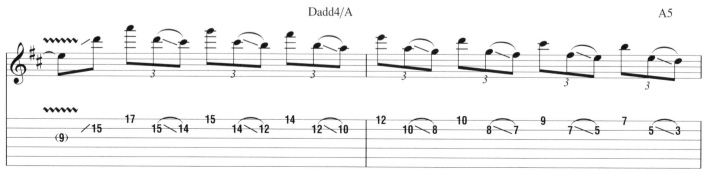

Dadd4/A   A5

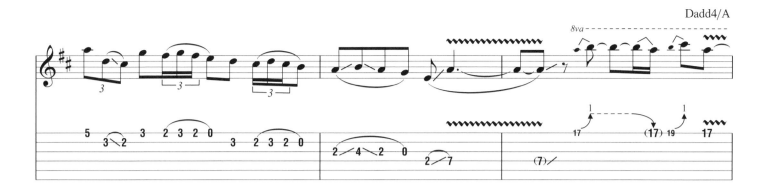

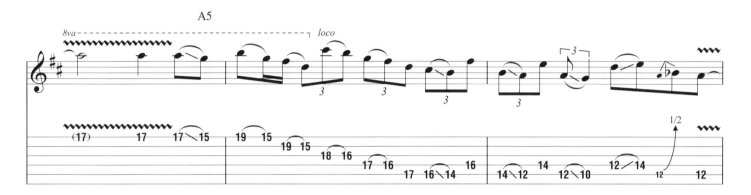

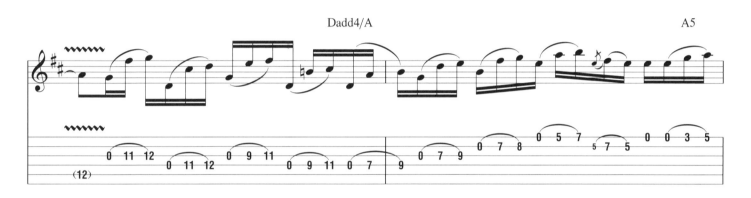

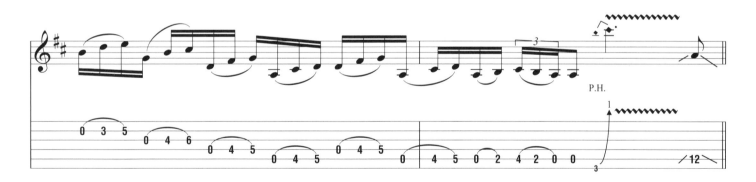

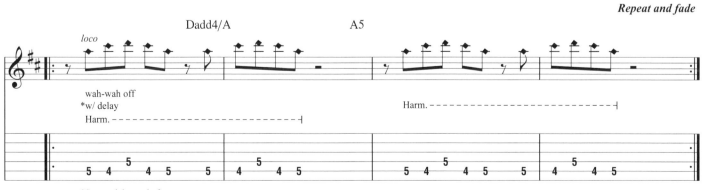

*Stereo delay as before.

Surfing With the Alien

By Joe Satriani

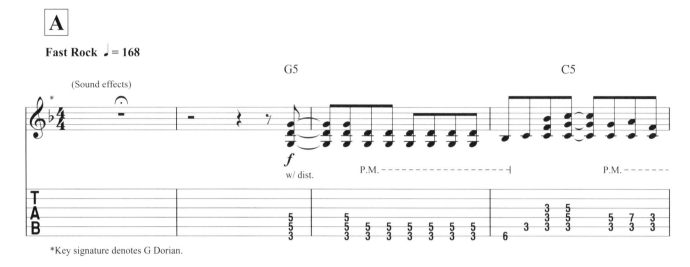

*Key signature denotes G Dorian.

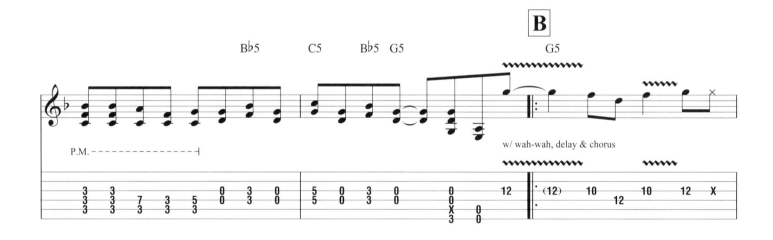

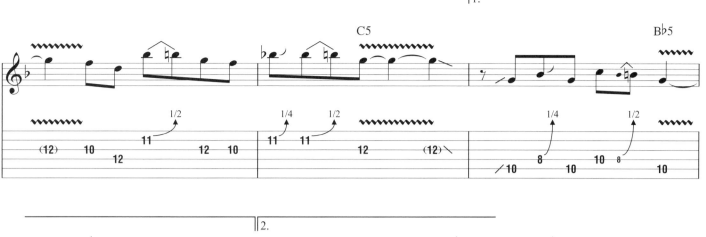
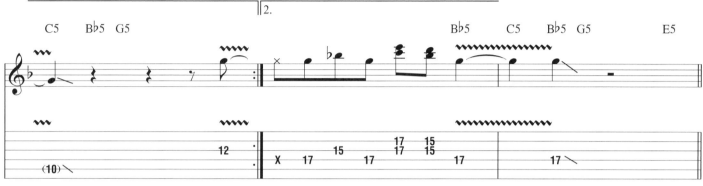
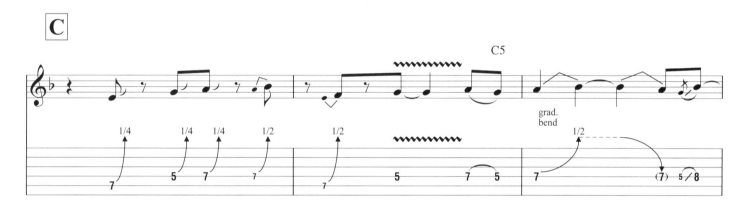
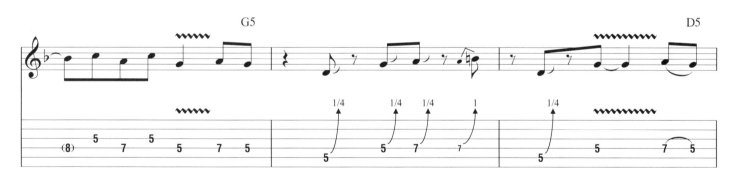
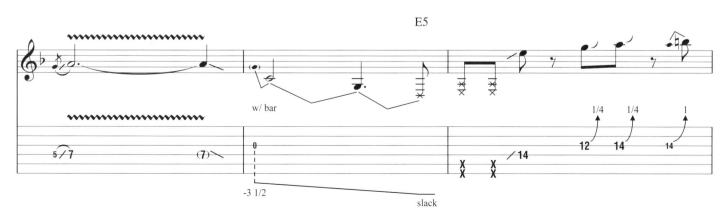

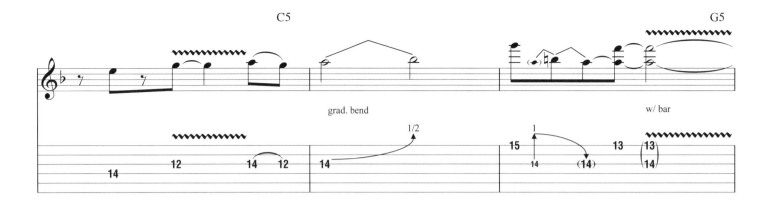

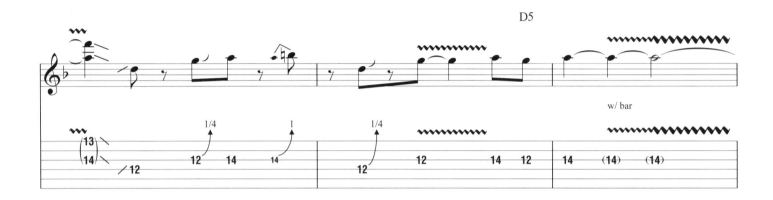

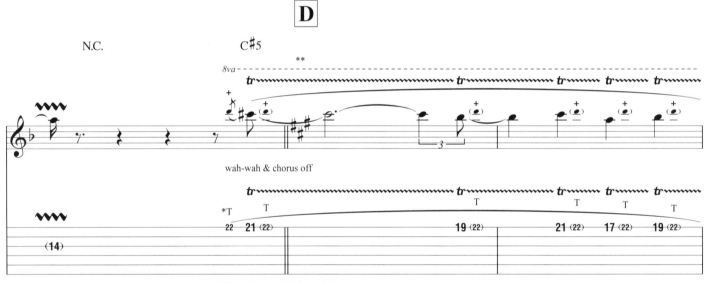

*Tap w/ edge of pick, next 5 meas.

**Key signature denotes C♯ Phrygian.

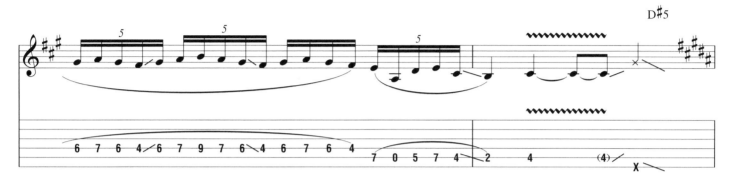

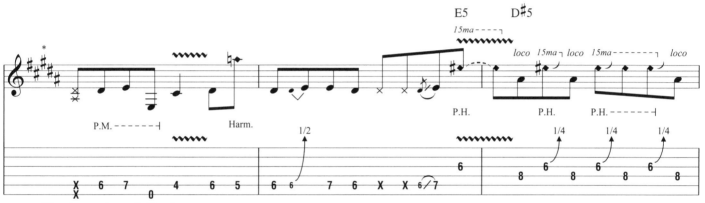

*Key signature denotes D# Phrygian.

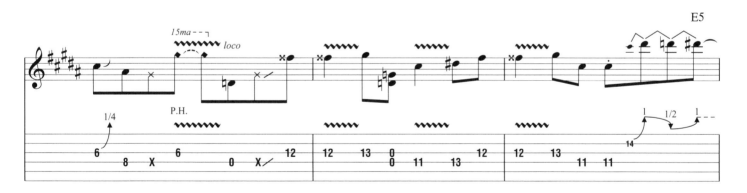

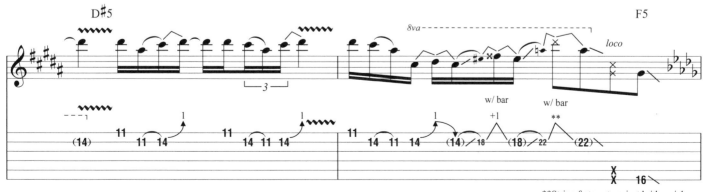

**String frets out against bridge pickup.

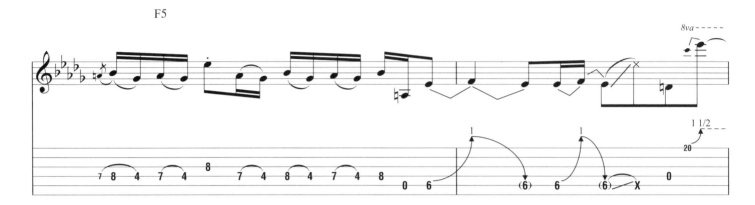

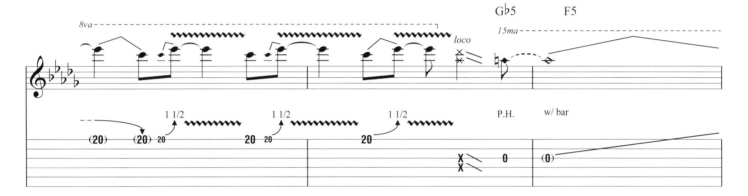

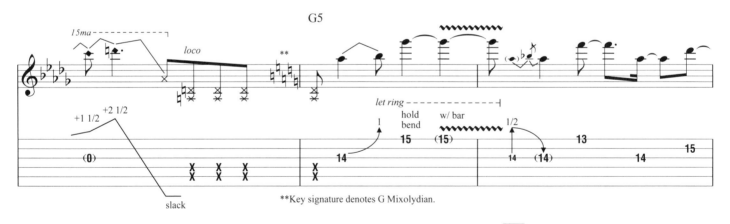

**Key signature denotes G Mixolydian.

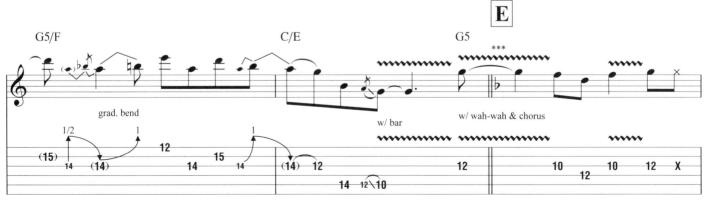

***Key signature denotes G Dorian.

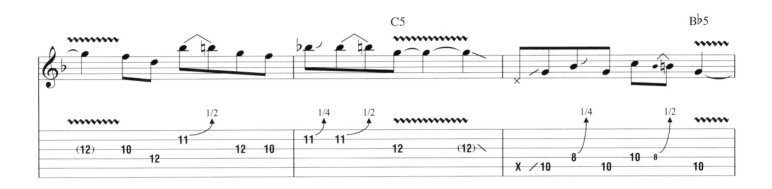

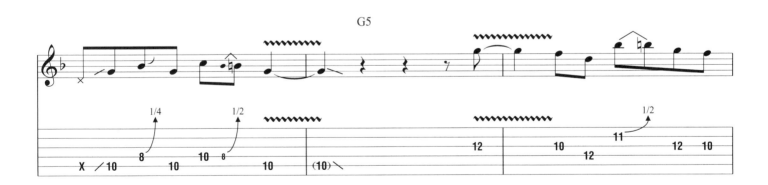

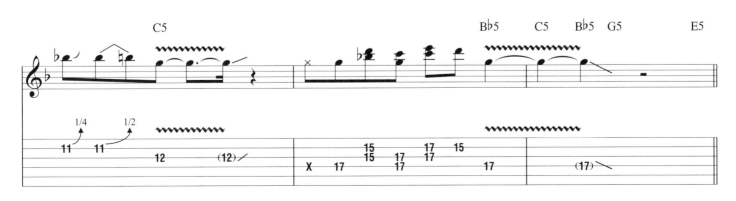

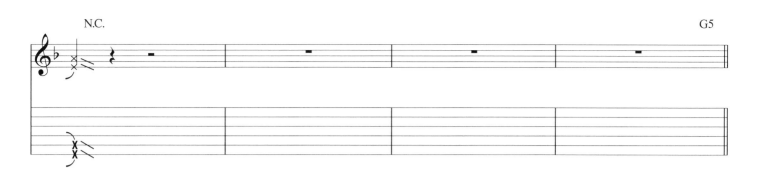

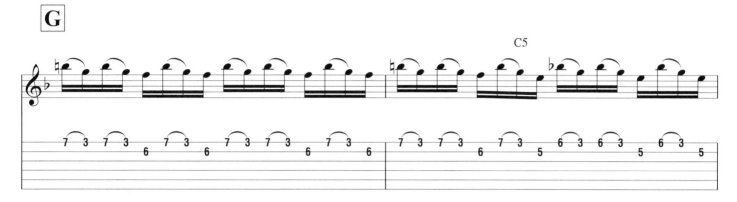

G

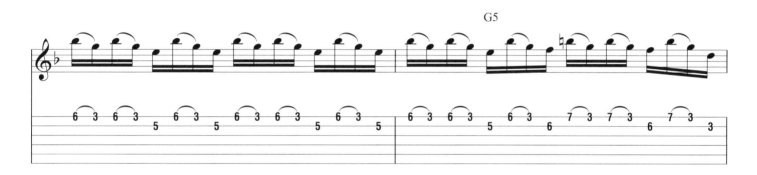

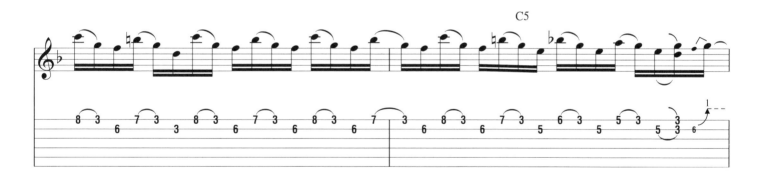

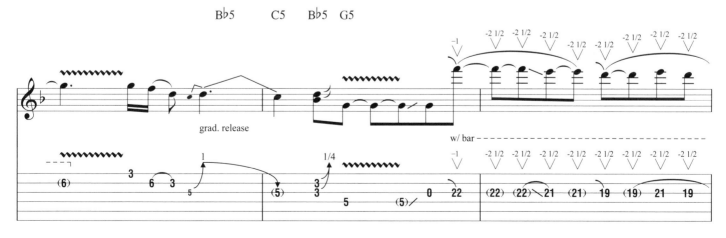

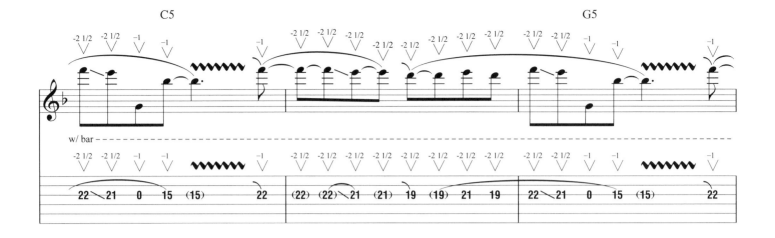

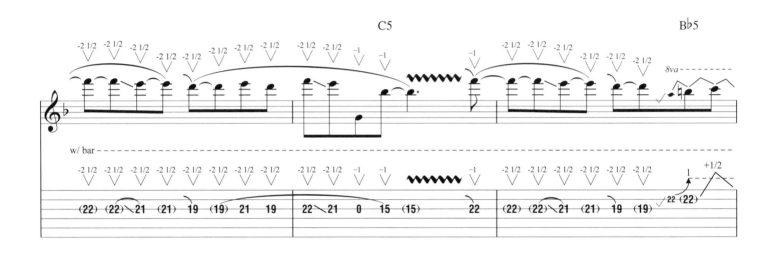

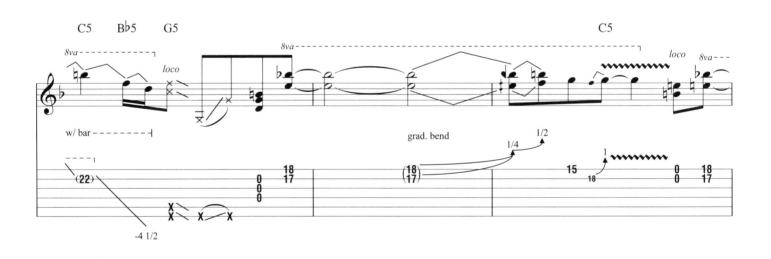

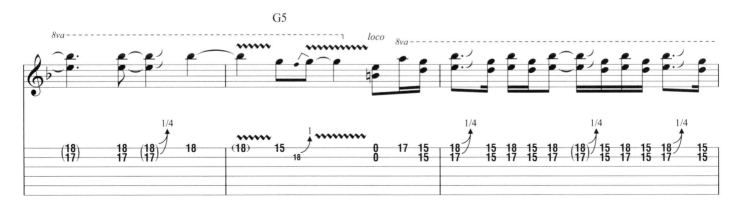

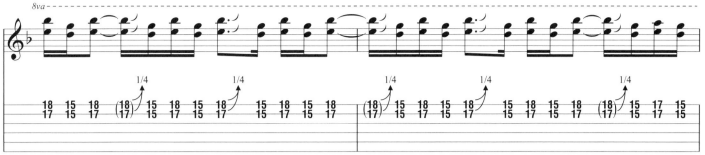

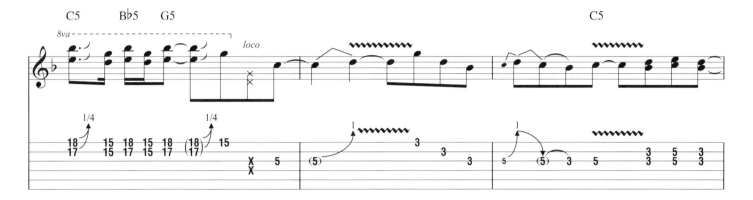

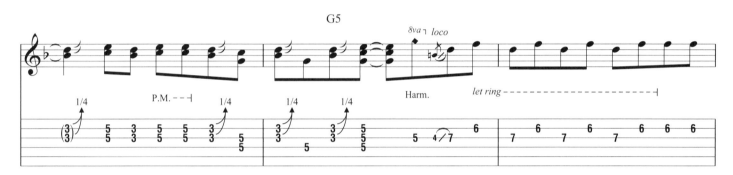

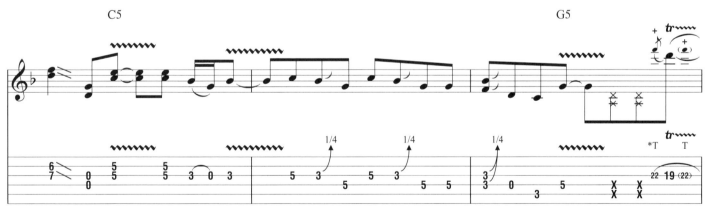

*Tap w/ edge of pick, next 4 meas.

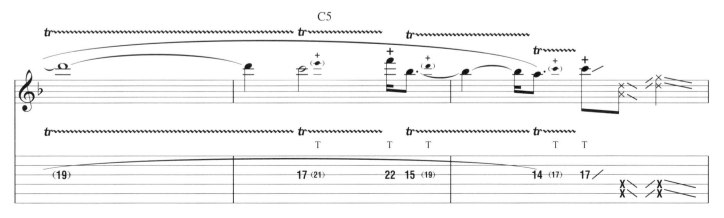

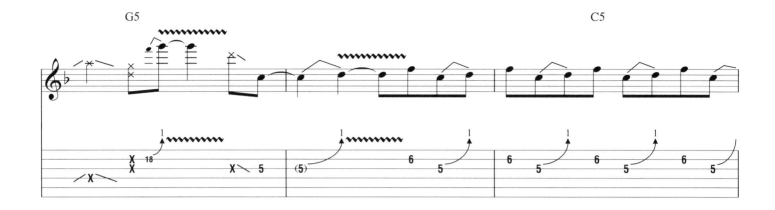

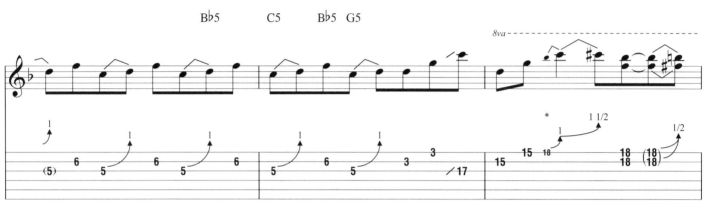

*Catch 2nd string w/ bending finger.

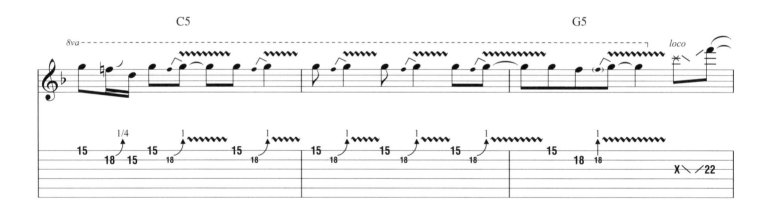

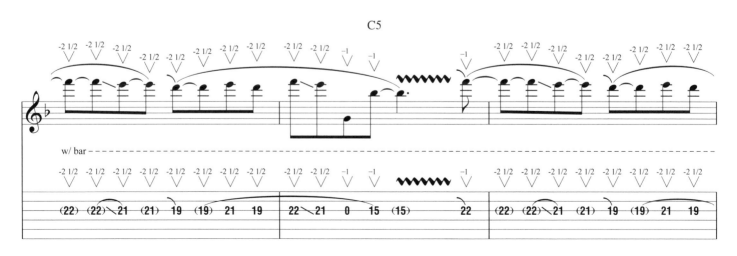

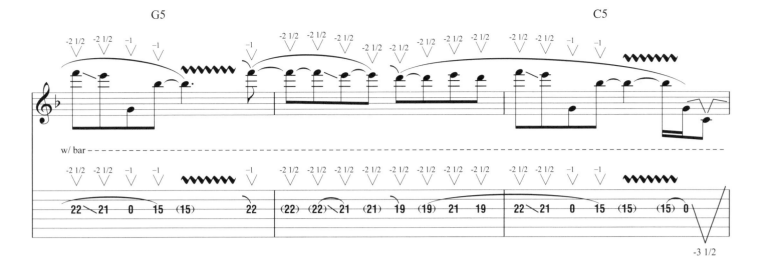

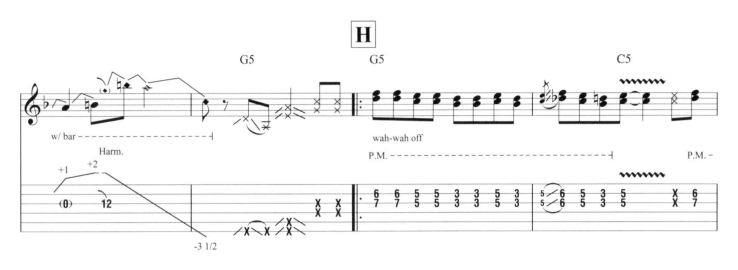

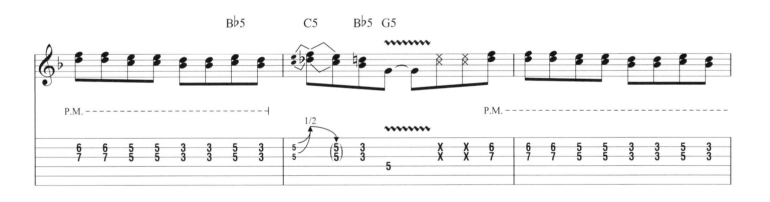

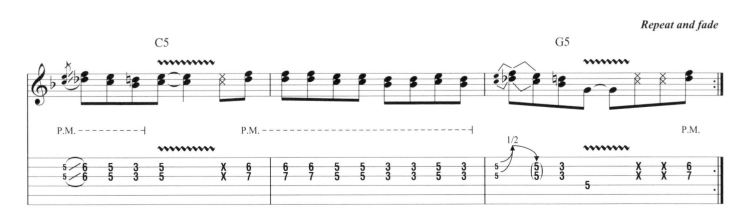

Starry Night

By Joe Satriani

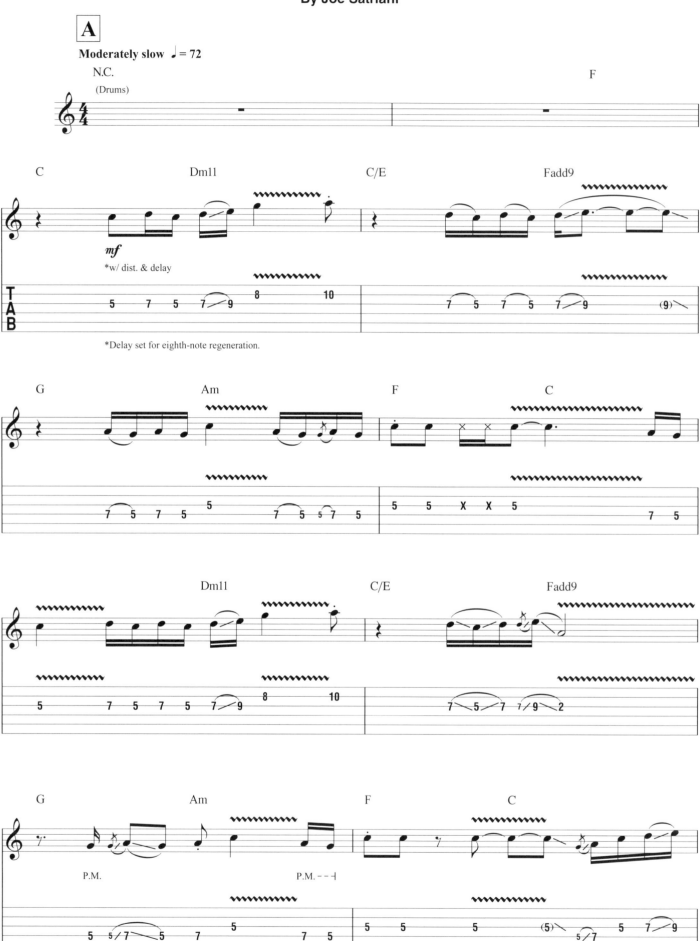

*Delay set for eighth-note regeneration.

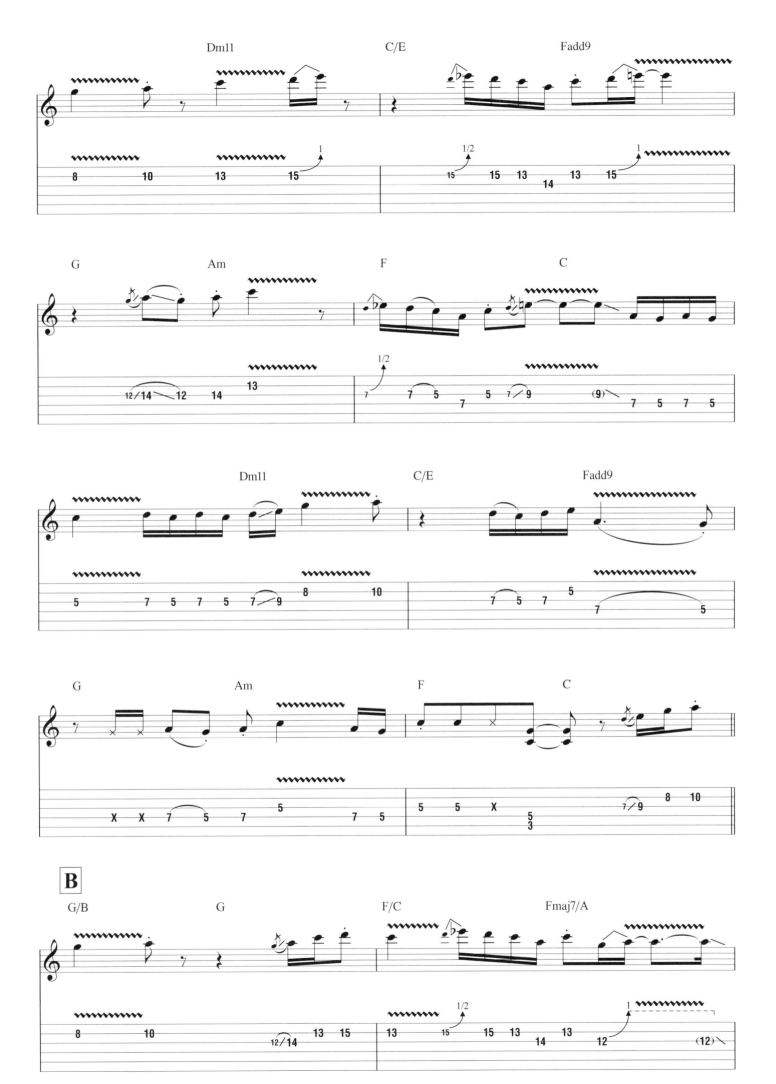

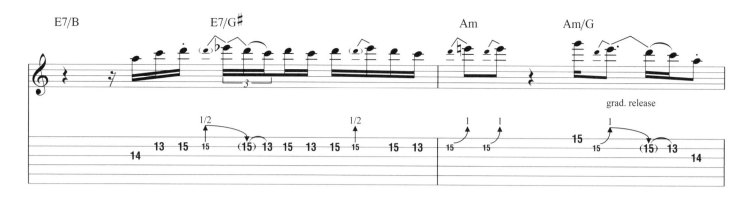

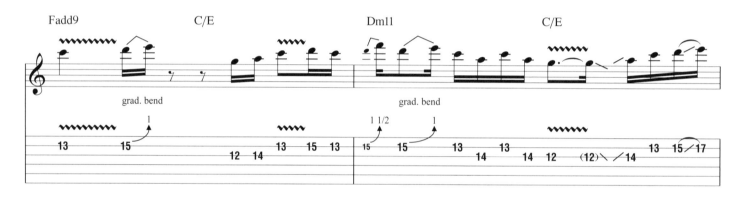

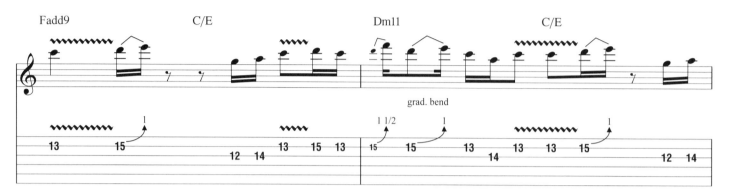

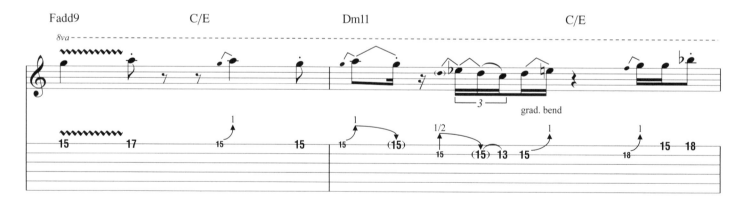

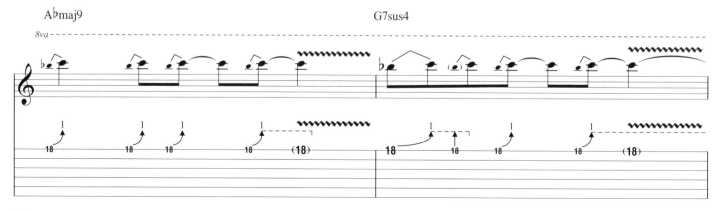

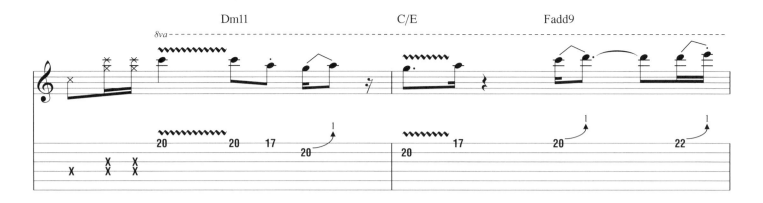

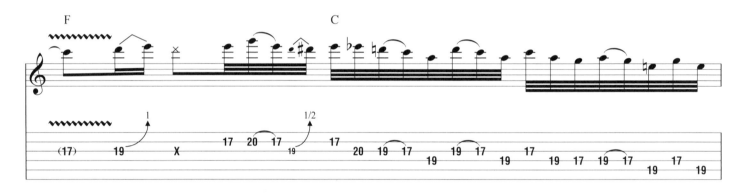

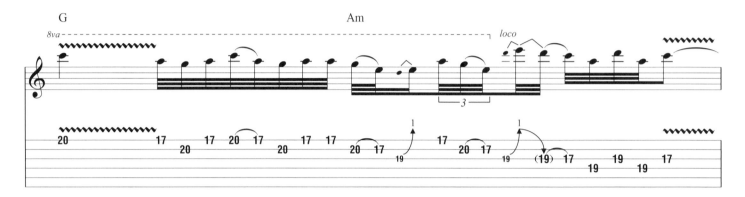

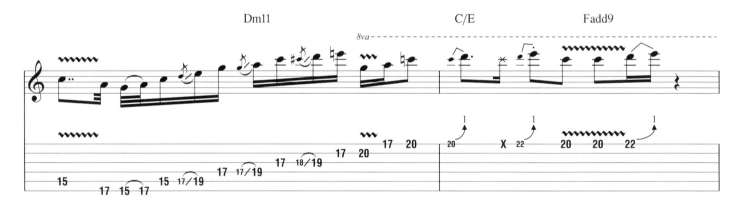

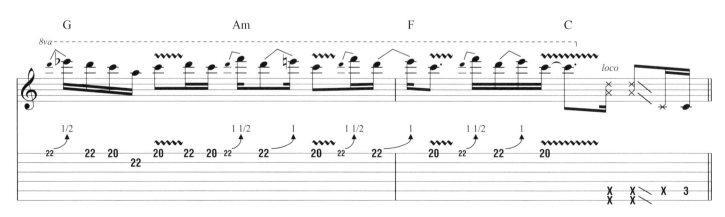

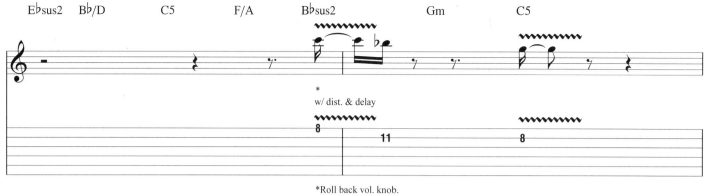

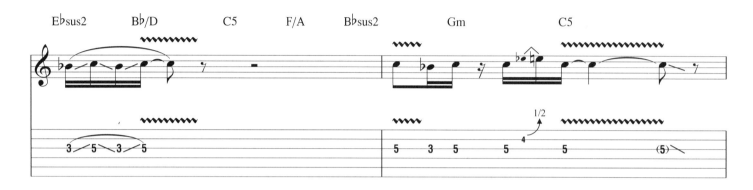

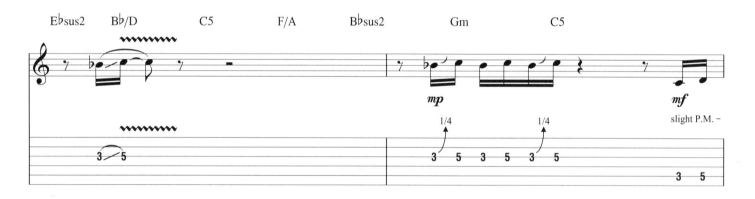

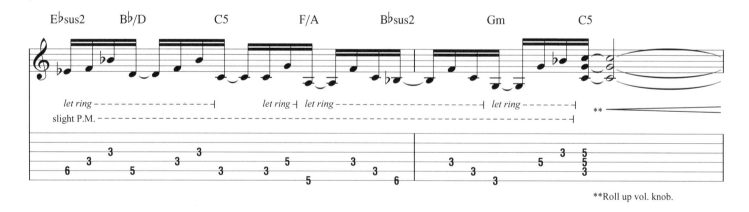

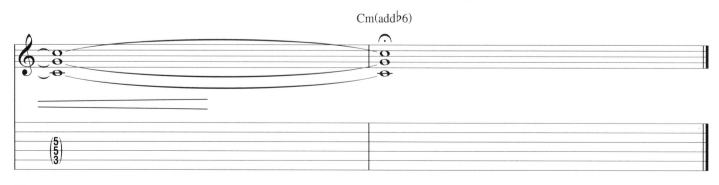